Losing Kay

Losing Kay

Living and Dying with Progressive Supranuclear Palsy

Keith Simmons

For Kay, our children, grandchildren and legion of friends

CONTENTS

CONTENTS

Introduction

We have had a wonderful life and this is just part of it.

We will take it a day at a time

On November 12, 2021, Kay Simmons died. She was my wife and best friend. Her death was a tragedy. She was too young, too full of life, and too much loved to have died when she did and as she did. She died of a degenerative brain disease that has been given the sterile, forgettable name progressive supranuclear palsy, or PSP for short. The disease when experienced in real time is neither sterile nor forgettable. It is a debilitating disease for which there is no treatment and no cure and always takes the life of its victim. The disease was cruel, draining, and unrelenting for Kay, while for those who loved and cared for her, it was physically, mentally, and emotionally exhausting.

At the time of her death at age seventy-two, Kay and I had been married for fifty years, five months, and fourteen days. We had had a great life together. Then, PSP struck. This is the story of our journey with the disease, as patient and caregiver, through love and loss, joy and sadness, death and dying.

Progressive supranuclear palsy is one of a handful of diseases, including corticobasal degeneration, multiple system atrophy, and fronto-temporal dementia that are classified as "atypical parkinsonisms." These diseases generally fall under the same umbrella as the commonly known condition Parkinson's disease, but the atypical parkinsonisms are different from Parkinson's disease in their physiology and consequences. The website CurePSP.org provides an excellent primer that is helpful in understanding PSP and its cousins.

We all have within our brains a protein called by medical science the "tau" protein. PSP is caused by the improper "folding" or "clumping" of the tau protein within neurons of the brain. When this occurs, cells in the affected area die without regeneration, resulting in a loss of function in that area.

No one seems to know why this occurs. The neurologists with whom we consulted along the way told us that there is no evidence that PSP is genetically transmitted or that it is caused by a virus or bacteria. The CurePSP.org website has some discussion about environmental factors, but really no one knows the cause. Inexplicably, it just happens. The brain just malfunctions. Nobody does or fails to do something to bring it on. It's just bad luck.

PSP doesn't occur often. The PSP website says the incidence of PSP is five out of one hundred thousand, meaning that, statistically, there are currently in our hometown of Nashville, Tennessee, thirty-five cases. If there are thirty-five cases in Nashville right now, I don't suppose you could say the disease is rare, but it is certainly unusual. If you have it, it is as real and usual as tomorrow morning's sunrise. If you have it, PSP becomes your life, your journey, and the journey of those around you.

As we started this journey, I sought others who have accompanied a loved one down this road. I found a few people who could give me some appreciation of the challenges to come and a little guidance in how to proceed, and I read a few firsthand accounts, but I never came upon a comprehensive account from start to finish. (After most of this narrative had been written, I discovered *Last Dance at the Savoy* by Kathryn Leigh Scott, whose husband died from PSP. Ms. Scott's account takes the reader through the experience of the author and her husband dealing with PSP. There may be others.)

If you are facing this disease, you may not want to know everything that lies ahead. Honestly, despite my intense efforts to understand the disease and discover what lay ahead of us, I am glad that I did not know it all. As much as I wanted to know in the moment what was next, I think I was better off just reacting. I think Kay was too. I think we probably suffered less just doing the best we could do under the circumstances, as circumstances arose and changed. But everyone is different. For someone who wants the full account in order to be prepared, here it is—the bad and the good, the sorrow and the joy, the anguish and the blessings. It is all here.

My experience as Kay's primary caregiver, in some ways, was no different than the experience of anyone caring for a loved one with one of those chronic, terminal diseases in our modern arsenal of suffering. Caregiving became my full-time job for the last three and a half years of Kay's life. I had the good fortune to be surrounded by a great, attentive family and wonderful engaged friends, but even with a great support system, the ultimate responsibility was on me. The decisions were mine to make, and Kay was unable to make them with me as she always had done. The physical and mental tolls were intense. Sometimes, I felt very, very alone.

Tom Coughlin, the two-time Super Bowl-winning head coach of the New York Giants, in his essay for the *New York Times* on August 24, 2021, shared his experience of caring for his wife who was afflicted with PSP. In "Nothing Could Prepare Me for Watching My Wife Slip Away," he writes, "I've learned firsthand caregiving is all-consuming. It is mentally and physically exhausting." At the end, he writes, "Don't forget about the caregivers." Ann Patchett, in her essay "My Three Fathers," published in *The New Yorker* on October 5, 2020, describes the work and responsibility undertaken by her stepmother, the primary caregiver for her father who died of PSP, as a "herculean" task. So my story is not only about PSP but also about caregiving and caregivers, whatever the disease might be. It is my homage to caregivers, whoever and wherever they are.

This is not a "how to." I have no advice for caregivers or sufferers of PSP. What worked for us or did not work for us will not be the same for others. I am just trying to describe our experience, the challenges that we faced, the decisions that we made, and all the emotions of the journey. Everyone is different and every journey is different. Every disease is different. Even every case of PSP is different. Life expectancy is different with each case of PSP, and the debilitating effects are different with each case. The tau protein has no preordained agenda. It just goes where it goes on its own timetable, and we are all, in some sense, just along for the ride. What the disease cannot take away from us as caregivers, however, is the discovery of the deep love and devotion that we can feel for our loved one and the indescribable love we can receive in return.

I don't know who might be my audience. Someone who might pick this up would not have to read it front to back, cover to cover. I have divided the story into parts. Some parts may be of interest and others not pertinent. The first part deals with Kay and who she was as a person. The body of the narrative deals specifically with the disease, Kay's early symptoms, her decline, the ways in which the disease affected her, and the way in which it took her life. Then I address the emotions that I went through as a caregiver, my experience finding a person or persons to help me care for Kay, the experience dealing with hospice, and the love bestowed on us by our friends and family. At the end, I write about grief, mourning, and loss, and finish with a reflection on her, on death, and on life without her.

The audience might be different for each part. The audience might be someone who has been newly diagnosed with PSP or is experiencing PSP-like symptoms or that person's loved ones. The audience may be a caregiver somewhere who is feeling alone, beleaguered, and out of gas. It may be a physician or other medical professional who knows the physiology, but not the reality of the disease. The audience may be the multitude of people who knew and loved Kay and do not want to forget the joy of their life with her. The audience may be someone dealing with grief and loss as I am. Or, my audience may be no one. It doesn't matter. This is for Kay and for me.

In my account of our life with PSP, I have tried to be very open about my rawest emotions as a caregiver and a grieving husband. In particular, the sections "Caregiving" and "Grief" are deeply personal. I needed to sort through my emotions and be honest with myself about how I felt. I suppose it was my way of processing grief and loss. I just could not bury my emotions. I needed to take all those feelings out, examine them, and give them a closer look.

But just as important as my own healing is my hope that some caregiver somewhere or someone grieving the loss of a loved one will see this. If you are that person, I hope you will read the sections on caregiving and grief to come to the knowledge that you are not alone in feeling the way you may feel. My emotions are not going to be your emotions. Just because I went through the anger, depression, sadness, and total array of emotions that I speak of here does not mean that your emotions will be the same. But I share my rawest, most intense emotions as best I can in order to validate your emotions whatever they are. Suppressing those emotions is a mistake. You are entitled to feel the way you feel.

A good friend once asked me if this narrative, then in its nascent state, would have a theme. I reflected on that question, as I revised the draft again and again. My initial intent had been to offer a chronicle of our experience with PSP so that others might benefit from it. I have not departed from that original purpose, but as I wrote and revised, I discovered that the story is far richer, nuanced, and involved than a simple narrative of the consequences of PSP. The theme is how disease and hardship cannot conquer the human spirit. Eclipsing the devastation of the disease and the telling of it is Kay's remarkable spirit in the face of the disease. In memorializing what we went through and what she went through, the extraordinary woman that was, and always will be, my wife was revealed anew. With every revision, I found emerging from each section, each paragraph, each sentence her remarkable courage, her resiliency, her boundless energy and interests, her love of family and friends, her desire to care for others even as they were caring for her, her love of life and all its aspects, her love of beautiful things—be they daffodils, dresses, art, or people—her love for me in the most trying of all times, and her triumph over death.

Over a period of approximately four and a half years, as her health slowly declined, she never lost her sense of humor, her mischievous nature, or her love of people. I don't think she ever felt sorry for herself. She was seldom depressed or angry. She just said, "We have had a wonderful life and this is just part of it. We will take it a day at a time." And she did. That is the theme. How could there be any other?

2

Who Was Kay?

Kay and I met on a double blind date in 1969. She was twenty and I was twenty-one. I was a college senior and she a college junior at the University of Kentucky in Lexington. Why was it a double blind date? Her roommate, Karen, was dating a guy who had a friend coming in from out of town for the weekend. This friend needed a date so he could go out with Karen and her boyfriend. Kay had had it with blind dates and did not want to go, but Karen, finally, wheedled out her consent. Then, at the eleventh hour, the out-of-town guy didn't show up. Who knows why? Whatever the reason, I became the default choice because I may have been the only guy on campus without a date on this, the first big football and party weekend of the year. If she did not want to go out with the out-of-town guy, how did she feel about the guy coming off the bench?

We went to the game. We had a great time. She went home and called her mother and told her she had met the guy she was going to marry. It was not my charm. It was Kay. That's how she was. When she knew, she knew. She was not the sort of coed who lacked for guys wanting to go out with her. She was rife with opportunities. As I discovered on our first night together, she was pretty—no, not just pretty. She was great-looking, smart, fun, and a joy to be with as a companion. But she knew, and eighteen months later, just as she predicted, we were married.

We married in 1971. The VietNam war was raging and every able-bodied male was subject to being conscripted into military service. I had an obligation to the United States Air Force, and upon being commissioned a Second Lieutenant, I was off to active duty. Fortunately, my duty assignment was not Saigon, but Ellsworth AFB in Rapid City, South Dakota, as an ICBM missile launch officer. Six months into my assignment, we were married and Kay joined me in South Dakota.

When we learned that we would be living in Rapid City, South Dakota, we had no idea where we were going. We had to look up Rapid City on the map. Western South Dakota is a beautiful part of the country, but in 1971, it was remote and isolated and no place for a brand-new female college graduate with a degree in public relations to start a career.

When we exchanged marital vows, she was not quite twenty-two years old and just three weeks out of college. While friends were seeking glamorous big-city jobs, she was following me to this remote, mysterious place to start her adult life. She loved me. She loved me enough to commit herself to what could potentially be four years in a place she had never seen before and knew nothing about with a guy she had known for eighteen months. She knew her own mind, never doubting that we would make a wonderful life for ourselves. That was Kay. She was special.

Since there were no public relations jobs in western South Dakota in 1971 for smart, young college graduates, especially female college graduates, I told Kay to take it easy. I was getting a regular paycheck for the first time in my life. I saw no immediate need for her to work. Yes, that was an embarrassingly sexist, condescending point of view, but it was 1971. That's my only excuse. I had a lot to learn, and she was going to teach me, however painful the lessons needed to be.

Soon, she had a job. Her job was to teach people how to floss their teeth. Her title was Dental Disease Control Educator. It was a horrible job, working for misogynistic dentists who told her that it was the best job in a four-state area. The unspoken appendage to that statement was "for a woman." She taught teeth cleaning without complaint while she took ceramics classes, created handmade Christmas ornaments, perfected her bridge skills, signed a letter of complaint to the Chair of Joint Chiefs of Staff, took care of our home and needs, and prepared dinner each night. I soon realized that maybe I had married a handful of energy, someone who was going to transform my life.

After military service, we found our way to Nashville, Tennessee, a place with more opportunity than western South Dakota. Kay began her professional life at Vanderbilt University in the Alumni and Development Office. She learned the art and skill of philanthropic fundraising and, with the hard work and creative energy she applied to every part of her life, she eventually became the preeminent development professional in the city. She could connect with people in a very special way. People liked her and she liked people. As I said in eulogizing her, "Men wanted to be with her; women wanted to be like her; and children loved her."

As our life together unfolded, Kay became a full-time mom, a full-time professional, a full-time friend to legions of people, and a full-time partner, friend, and spouse to me. She even took up politics for a time and succeeded at that as well. She fixed a home-cooked dinner for our family every night and insisted that our little family of five sit at the same table, without distractions, to enjoy the food and each other. She maintained an exhausting social life, learned gardening, modern dance, flower arranging, and smocking, and stayed fit with swimming, walking, running, and any other activity that satisfied her desire for action and friendships. She had a network of friends who came to know each other because they were in her orbit. She was a woman of unlimited energy—physical energy, creative energy, relational energy, and passionate energy.

She was a force of nature and continued to be throughout her life, even when the terrible disease that took her life began to gnaw away at her.

We were blessed with three healthy, bright, well-adjusted children who have grown into adulthood and become parents and spouses as well. Jennifer is our firstborn. She is a lawyer, like her dad, only better; the mother of three boys; and wife to Daniel. Lauren, our middle child, is married to Brian. Lauren was a world-class middle-distance runner in college and after college. She and Brian have three children, two girls and a boy. Lauren has a master's degree in social work and conducts a thriving counseling practice. Our youngest child, Barton, is married to Hayley. They have three little girls. He was an outstanding athlete throughout high school and college and now enjoys a career in college football recruiting circles. As of this writing and at the time Kay died, all three of our children and their families, including all nine grandchildren, live in Nashville within ten minutes of our house. Kay was healthy, engaged with her family and community, and poised to live for many more years until PSP struck. Nobody had it better than we had it. We had been supremely blessed for our entire life together.

Kay's impact on the community of Nashville is remarkable and beyond debate. She was the founding executive director of three significant nonprofit foundations, supporting the Vanderbilt Medical Center, the Vanderbilt Law School, and Nashville Public Schools, respectively. She found her real passion—primary and secondary school education—when she took the position as Director of Development of the University School of Nashville, a prestigious K–12 independent school. She even served as the school's interim head for a year with no formal training as an educator. She could get things done and manage people and programs, and the school's board recognized those talents despite her lack of credentials.

As her career evolved, she refocused her passion for education on public school education, serving as the founding executive director of the Nashville Public Education Foundation. She passionately cared about children and wanted to do all in her power to ensure a quality education for all children.

Kay was not political by nature, but she had an embedded sense of right and wrong. She campaigned for and was elected to the Metropolitan Nashville Public Schools Board of Education because she thought she could make a difference in Nashville's public schools. She campaigned door-to-door in the New Hampshire winter for Al Gore to be elected president because she thought it was the right thing to do. She took on a battle with the Tennessee Secondary School Athletic Association. Girls' basketball games as a preliminary to the boys' games in Tennessee were a long-standing tradition in high school basketball. Kay thought this was wrong on two counts. One, it made the girls' games seem less important than the boys'. And two, all the games were played in the evenings, which made it difficult for parents to get from work to the games in time to see their daughters play. Over the TSSAA's resistance, Kay succeeded for a time in changing this tradition for games played at University School.

She took in strangers and helped the marginalized. We hosted over twenty foreign exchange students in our home during our life together, some for only a couple of weeks and some for as long as two years. She took in strangers to live in our basement bedroom when they needed a place to stay. She once happened upon someone with small children at home who was undergoing radiation treatments and needed a place to stay during the treatments. Kay domiciled her in the basement bedroom for two weeks. Our kids, teenagers and preteens at the time, referred to her as the "radioactive lady" living with us. Kay also befriended a refugee couple from Kosovo and a refugee family from Azerbaijan. She served as a Big Sister in the Big Brothers, Big Sisters program. Even after she contracted PSP, she and her friend Anne took weekly trips to the state prison to visit and brighten the life of Andrew, a death row inmate. There was no limit to her energy and her good work.

Since Kay's death, I have devoted hours to accepting and acknowledging accolades for her contributions to our community. The irony of these acknowledgments is that she never sought recognition for any-thing she did. For her, it was about people and the need. Her mantra was "See it, do it." If she saw something that needed fixing, she would fix it. If she saw something that needed to be done, she would do it. Her taking was a tragedy for her, for me, for her children, her grandchildren, her legion of friends, and the community in which we have lived for forty-nine years.

My description of her would not be complete without emphasizing how pretty she was. She had dark hair and dark eyes and a skin tone that bronzed in the summer. She was a head-turner when we married, not just to me but to everyone, and she never seemed to age. She was always beautiful, always a head-turner. Even after PSP came to visit, she maintained her glow until her last days.

Kay had an impeccable sense of style. She knew exactly how to dress just right for every occasion. She enjoyed dressy affairs, and we went to a lot of them. Often, when we were ready to walk out the door to some event, I would glance at her, charmed anew, and say, "Wow, you look great!" Eric Clapton may have said it better, "Yes, you look wonderful tonight." She always did.

3

The Early Signs of PSP

Sure, We Can Do That

The starting point for some diseases can be pinpointed, allowing the progression to be tracked and even predicted. That is not so for PSP. We don't know when it started in Kay. It crept up on us with the stealth of a cat. We didn't know she had it until its malevolent work was well underway. At some point, Kay's brain cells began to die without regeneration, but in those early days, the changes in her were almost imperceptible.

In hindsight, knowing now what lay ahead, we can find hints of early decline. Our daughter Jennifer thinks she saw signs of decline as early as May 2015, when she and Daniel moved to a bigger house to accommodate their growing family. Jennifer naturally thought her mom, an inveterate multitasker and adept organizer, would apply all her skills in helping her and her family settle into their new home. To Jennifer's surprise, Kay showed no interest in organizing and seemed incapable of multitasking. Jennifer wrote it off at the time to advancing age. Looking back on it now, she believes Kay may have been showing signs of the disease even then—three years before she was diagnosed and six and a half years before it took her life.

In April 2016, Kay and I moved to the house in which I currently live, the house in which she died. A small group of friends gathered to help her get settled. Looking back, her friends now say that she was not her usual efficient, industrious, organized self.

In May of 2016, Kay and I went to Italy with our friends Bitsy and Wearen. Bitsy noticed on that trip that Kay was not totally herself. Even though the trip was a great success, and all of us, including Kay, had a wonderful time, Bitsy thought Kay was a bit withdrawn and not as engaged and gregarious as usual. She also thought Kay seemed confused at times. Bitsy recalls one time when we were in a rental car together, with Kay in the front passenger seat in charge of the radio and navigation, that Kay could not figure out the radio. Even to an American in Italy, it was not complicated. Now that we know what unfolded later, it is easy to apply a revisionist gloss to what seemed at the time to be innocuous actions and events, but Bitsy's observations carry no such gloss. She was concerned enough at the time, without the benefit of knowing what was to come, to confide to a friend upon our return that Kay did not seem fully herself.

Kay retired at the end of 2011 from full-time professional activities, but she continued to get calls from nonprofits to advise on fundraising strategies. She said yes to some of these requests and began a modest consulting practice, limiting her commitments so that we could travel and be grandparents. In the spring of 2016, she began advising Nashville Public Radio. At some point during her engagement with NPR, word drifted back to Kay's sister Pat that the consulting wasn't going well. In board meetings, she couldn't put sentences together and be coherent. She eventually parted with NPR, saying that the CEO did not want to do the hard work of asking for money. I wonder now if there was more to it.

As early as 2014, Kay had been conducting a monthly book club for the Osher Lifelong Learning Institute at Vanderbilt University. I was not a part of the book club, but sometime in 2016, I was interested in the book up for discussion and went to that meeting. I recall noticing how uncharacteristically passive and disengaged she seemed as the leader of the discussion. I was concerned that others would notice her seeming diffidence and started going to all the meetings to help with the discussion. At the time, I didn't think of it as covering for her, but clearly she was not herself, and whether or not I recognized it at the time, I was covering for her.

Looking back on those days, I was slower than others to recognize, or perhaps accept, that something had changed in her. I was with her every day and these changes were subtle and slow moving. I think I was just subconsciously adjusting daily to what I perceived to be the aging process in both of us.

It must have been sometime in 2016 when Kay's sister-in-law, Cathy, came to her in private and suggested to her that something was wrong. Cathy had noticed that Kay was not pronouncing words correctly and not translating thoughts to words as well as she should. She was also seeing, like Bitsy, that Kay appeared to be less engaged and a little confused at times. Cathy says now that she noticed changes as early as 2014. I think it is debatable whether Kay was showing signs of the disease that early, over seven years before she died, but Cathy was concerned enough in 2016 to take the extraordinary step of having a difficult conversation with Kay.

After their conversation, Kay came to me and told me what Cathy had said. She wanted to know my observations. I said that I didn't see anything wrong with her, but after that conversation, I began to pay more attention to her actions and behavior. I also began to notice her slurring certain words. I still didn't become overly concerned as she had always mispronounced some words. I wrote it off to genetics and advancing age. Her father had always slightly mispronounced some words in that same way. Maybe I was just rationalizing my way around confronting the reality that she had something wrong with her.

At about the same time, I began to notice her propensity to hold her right hand at an upward angle. In mid-2016, Kay and I were regular afternoon babysitters for three of our grandchildren. Occasionally, we would take them from their house to Jenni's Ice Cream, some four or five blocks away. One day, as we were headed home from Jenni's, Kay was pushing the stroller with two of the grandchildren in it. I was following her, carrying the third child. The sidewalk was uneven and she tripped. I don't think the fall was related to PSP, but she drove the middle finger on her right hand into the sidewalk and damaged it badly. After the incident, she carried her right hand at an uplifted angle. She continued to do so even after the finger injury had healed. It was a harbinger of later disability and eventual loss of use of that hand.

In November and December of 2016, Kay had cataract surgery. Having worn either glasses or contacts since she was a teenager, she was excited about the surgery. She was expecting to be able to see both distance and close up without glasses or contacts, but the surgery didn't go well. She could see at a distance, but the vision was not at the level she had anticipated, and she still needed glasses for reading. Her doctor couldn't figure out what had gone wrong. Looking back on it now, I think she was probably experiencing the early effects of PSP.

Kay was one of the early board members of the Maddox Foundation, a prestigious foundation that makes annual charitable grants. She served continuously from 2012 through the end of 2018, chairing the board in 2015. The executive director of the foundation recalls that Kay, while speaking on behalf of the foundation at an event at Belmont University in 2015, seemed to search for words that came slowly and with some labor. Kaki, the executive director, like all of us, didn't know what to make of it at the time and thought nothing more of it.

Kaki also noticed in 2017 and 2018, toward the end of Kay's tenure on the Maddox board, that she arrived late to meetings and didn't follow all the conversation around the table. She sometimes worried that Kay might get lost on the way home. Of course, by this time, we knew something was wrong, and for some of that time I was taking her to meetings. That's probably why she was habitually late. Even though the disease had progressed significantly by the end of Kay's tenure on the board and was beginning to show itself in some of her actions and behavior, Kaki says that Kay could still offer keen insights and ask probing questions. The disease had bored in on her speech, dexterity, and personality, yet it left intact her ability to think in a very nuanced and incisive way.

Even though symptoms of the disease may have been creeping in as early as 2016, even 2015, we enjoyed an active travel life in those years. In addition to the aforementioned trip to Italy, we traveled to Cuba; Charleston, South Carolina; Washington, DC; Williamsburg, Virginia; and Ponte Vedra, Florida. We own a beach home in a development called Rosemary Beach, located in the panhandle of Florida on the Gulf of Mexico, and were there multiple times in 2015 and 2016. Kay served on the board of the International Storytelling Center, and traveled quarterly from our home in Nashville for board meetings in Jonesborough, Tennessee, five hours away. In October of both years, we attended the International Storytelling Festival in Jonesborough.

In the year 2015, a political year in Nashville, our mayor of the previous eight years was approaching the end of his second and final term. As a large field of contenders emerged and campaigns revved up, Kay's friend Linda announced her candidacy. Linda had never run for political office. She had spent her career in the technology and business world. Linda and Kay, in some ways, were cut from the same cloth. Linda is smart, energetic, creative, gets things done, and has a cheery, positive personality. Also, Linda had been one of Kay's most ardent supporters when Kay had been elected to the Metro Nashville Board of Education as previously noted. As the campaign unfolded, Linda asked Kay to take a paid position in her campaign. She said she needed an adult in the room to direct all the twentysomethings who gravitated toward the excitement of a political campaign. Kay took the job and became the de facto operations manager for a very high level political campaign. Linda did not win, but Kay's executive functions were still revving at that point even though signs of trouble may have been emerging otherwise.

The year 2016 marked the fortieth year since my graduation from Vanderbilt Law School. The reunion chair contacted us early that year and asked if we would host the Class of 1976 reunion party in October.

I am sure that he called us because he knew Kay would do it and do it well. By then, we had downsized to our current house, with less space for a big party. Undaunted, Kay said, "Sure, we can do that." And, we did, or more accurately, she did. A gathering of a group of sexagenerian and septuagenarian lawyers and judges has the potential to be a very dull party. In years past, the gatherings had lived up to their potential. Kay, refusing to have a dull party, set her goal on spicing it up. She found a Beatles cover band that sounded more like the Beatles than the Beatles and, over my skepticism, set them up in our living room. The result was a rollicking good time. She managed all that and pulled it off in her normal impressive way. Her organizational skills were still alive in 2016.

In January 2017, we went to Mexico to see the monarch butterfly sanctuary and visit Mexico City. The trip involved walking, climbing, sleeping in an unheated mountain room with a cold shower, riding a horse up a steep mountain trail, and braving various harrowing modes of transportation. The trip turned into a marvelous experience. We both loved it.

Reflecting on these years, it is really hard to pin down when PSP started. In hindsight, our daily lives were quite normal. Those years were wonderful even though the disease was starting to take hold. As abundantly clear from all our activities in those years and all the responsibility that she assumed during that time, she was still herself in many ways.

What was Kay perceiving in herself at this point? Describing her condition to the Mayo Clinic doctor who diagnosed her condition in 2018, she said, "The first hint of trouble, which was only appreciated in retrospect, was a generalized slowing and loss of former identity as a 'force of nature' about four years ago." That would have put the beginning date sometime in 2014. She also said to the doctor, "Two years ago, others started to notice a change in my voice, including softening and slurring." She was certainly correct about the voice issues beginning in 2016. I have looked at her handwriting in 2016, and found it to have declined noticeably by that time.

Was she suffering from the disease in 2014, four years before she was diagnosed and over seven years before she died? I doubt it. I think she may have been engaging in revisionist history herself. But maybe, just maybe, she was seeing it then—not knowing what to make of it and not sharing it with anyone. If so, that makes me very sad. When she began visibly and knowingly suffering from the disease, she was suffering with an enormous support system. But was she noticing changes in herself much earlier, being anxious about them, and not sharing her anxiety with me or others? Was she confronting the disease alone without her support network? I pray that was not happening.

PSP moves along at its unrelenting, inexorable pace. Nothing stops it or changes its trajectory. That is the tortuous part of PSP, but this plodding pace also gave her time to savor life and love her friends, her children, and especially her grandchildren. Even as it progressed, it gave her time to adjust to each new phase of life that the disease handed her, and it gave those of us around her, who loved her so much, time to adjust as well and cherish our time with her.

As we have gone through this experience, I have been impressed both by how much doctors and scientists know about the brain and how much they don't know. The maddening thing about PSP is not being able to know when it started, what causes it, or how to predict its trajectory. Not knowing makes it hard. Did she have it for seven years? That is closer to the normal life span that appears in the medical literature than three and a half years, her life span from diagnosis, or four and a half, the time from when the symptoms became obvious. I repeatedly asked the neurologists, "How long does she have to live?" "What is next?" I always got the same answer—a shrug of the shoulders.

4

What Was Next

I'd trade all my tomorrows for a single yesterday

"Me and Bobby McGee"—Kris Kristofferson

The watershed event that started us down the road to neurological testing and doctor visits occurred over Independence Day weekend 2017. The extended family had been with us at Rosemary Beach for the holiday itself, but Kay and I stayed on after they left. At some point, we decided to go biking. I got the bicycles out of storage. We strapped on our helmets and started to mount the bikes. I had my back to her when I heard a thud. She had fallen headfirst as she was mounting her bike.

For a brief moment, she seemed to lose consciousness. It was really scary. If she had not been wearing a helmet, she would have suffered a concussion. I was able to get her up. She was briefly disoriented, but quickly regained her senses. She hurt her head and knees, but not her hands, indicating a possible blackout either as or perhaps before she fell. In any case, there was no evidence that she had tried to catch herself. Oddly, she had never blacked out like that before, and it never happened again. Nevertheless, the absence of any damage to her palms was curious. I don't think the fall was PSP induced, but balance would become one of her central issues in the ensuing months. Could the fall have been an early sign of PSP? We will never know. What we do know is what came next.

We didn't go to a doctor in Florida, but when we came home we called her primary care physician, Dr. Jennifer Green. Dr. Green ordered a CT scan of her head and face and an X-ray of her knee, all of which occurred on July 17, 2017. The results revealed nothing abnormal.

In early August, Kay experienced persistent light-headedness for about a week. With no relief by the end of the week, we called Dr. Green, who told us to go to the emergency room, get an MRI of Kay's brain, and go now. So, on Friday, August 11, 2017, we found ourselves in the emergency room of the Vanderbilt Medical Center. We arrived sometime in the late afternoon. It was one of those experiences that gives emergency rooms a bad name. We did not get home until dawn.

We were seen first by a young doctor, who appeared at first glance to have recently graduated from eighth grade. I immediately figured out that he was smarter than any eighth grader whom I had ever met, and perhaps smarter than anyone of any age whom I had ever met. He ordered an MRI of her head. I think he probably suspected a brain tumor or some sort of residual trauma from the fall. We had to wait our turn. In the meantime, the Vanderbilt ER was at capacity, meaning that we were positioned in a hallway, sitting and lying on a gurney where we spent the night. Finally, at about 9:00 p.m., two officious technicians came for her. My job was to ask enough questions of those guys to be sure they had the right patient and that she was not heading to the amputation room. Sitting in the Vanderbilt ER for five hours seemed like an eternity, but I would gladly sit on a gurney there every night for the rest of my life if I could just do it with her.

A couple of hours after Kay's MRI, the young doctor reappeared and said the MRI was showing nothing abnormal, but that something was creating the light-headedness. He suggested that he order an MRI of her spine. This conversation occurred at roughly 11:00 p.m. She actually went into the MRI tube at 4:46 a.m. on the twelfth. As I now read the results of the test on the Vanderbilt patient portal, I am struck by the words "essentially unremarkable cervical spine MRI." But something was going on that was not "unremarkable." Our lives never again would be "unremarkable."

I do not remember that the light-headedness persisted, but in the clinical notes from our much later visit to Mayo Clinic, the Mayo doctor memorialized what Kay said to him as follows: "The light-headedness has continued to fluctuate, tending to occur in the seated or standing positions at any time of the day, made worse by looking up or down or rapidly changing her direction of gaze."

We saw Dr. Green again a week after the ER experience. She was concerned enough about Kay's condition to refer her to a neuropsychologist at the Cognitive and Behavioral Clinic at Vanderbilt who works with patients with head traumas, memory and cognitive issues, or early stage Alzheimer's or dementia. We only met with her once. After the visit with the neuropsychologist, Kay started seeing the physical therapists at the Bill Wilkerson Center at the Pi Beta Phi Institute at Vanderbilt to work on her balance.

In August 2017, a month after the fall in Florida, Kay and I attended her fiftieth high school reunion in Louisville. The first night, Friday night, was limited to graduates only. Spouses were included the second night. We drove to Louisville on Friday and arrived about the time her classmates were arriving. I dropped her off at the event, made sure she was where she was supposed to be, and left. Linda, one of her best friends in high school, was in attendance and saw a lot of Kay that night. As the party unfolded, Linda noticed something was wrong with Kay. She kept asking Linda, "Who are these people?"

We were spending the night with Kay's sister Susan that night. While Kay was attending the grads-only event, Susan and I went to dinner together. We talked about Kay a lot that night. We were both becoming concerned about her. I was concerned primarily about the balance issues and the light-headedness. Susan was seeing much more than I was. She was noticing her slurring of speech and personality changes. It was one of the first times that a family member really bored in on me about Kay's condition. I think I was still in denial, but Susan was not and I don't think others were either.

On the second night of the reunion, spouses were included. Normally, in an environment like her high school reunion, Kay would have been talking to everyone, moving effortlessly through the crowd, chatting and having fun. That night, she clung to me. I would say to her that she should go be with her friends. She preferred just to hold onto me as if she were a stranger in a strange environment or as if she was just a very shy, meek, diffident person, which of course she was not. Linda said later that she also observed Kay was quieter than usual that evening and wasn't as engaged and animated as usual. Others who noticed it came to Linda later and asked what was wrong with Kay. Linda reminded me much later that, in conversation, I would fill in whenever Kay would have trouble expressing herself. I was protecting her without fully knowing what I was doing.

Through the fall of 2017, she continued to have some coordination and speech issues. In September, she came to me one day in frustration because she was having trouble peeling an apple. She was losing the use of her right hand, her dominant hand, making even simple daily chores a challenge. She seldom cried about anything. But that day she cried. She knew something was wrong.

She was still mostly independent, but PSP was starting to make itself known. The upward carriage of her right hand was becoming more pronounced. Because of the declining ability to use her right hand, typing and writing were becoming harder. Even manipulation of eating utensils was becoming a challenge. Sometimes with atypical parkinsonisms, the patient will get an alien hand, a condition in which the hand develops a mind of its own and can actually be somewhat destructive. She never had that. Her difficulties were in simple dexterity. We feared for her condition, but we were getting no answers from the doctors. We could only guess at what was happening to her. It was a disconcerting time that we handled in the most positive, optimistic way that we could.

She saw a physical therapist weekly at the Pi Beta Phi to work on balance in the fall of 2017. But as diminished dexterity with her right hand began to show itself, we also began to see a therapist for that. The dexterity therapist had various tools for Kay to use to help her perform routine daily tasks of life, such as spoons and forks with abnormally large handles to make eating easier, and a yoke to put around a pen to help with writing. Of course, neither the doctors nor the physical therapists had any idea what they were treating. They were trying to ameliorate symptoms rather than treat the disease.

Kay worked hard at all the therapy exercises, and she did it with good humor. She had always been careful to take care of her health. After she died, I noticed a Redweld folder under her desk, marked "My Health," which contained a variety of physical therapy and medical notes. She did not want to be sick, and she certainly did not want to be sick because of her own inattention to her health. Throughout this phase, when we did not know what was wrong and anxiety and apprehension would have been natural in her, she went about her life as best she could, attacking the therapy sessions and resultant homework with the resolve that characterized everything she did.

We continued to take walks. When she had been healthy, I had a hard time keeping up with her on walks. By the fall of 2017, I would have to slow down so she could keep up with me. In hindsight, I think she walked more slowly because she was beginning to have trouble with her balance. She would fall sometimes, not in the really self-destructive way that was to come, but in a way indicating she was less steady on her feet. Her medical records indicate she went to the Vanderbilt Walk-In Clinic in late November of 2017 for a lacerated lip. I have no recollection of what happened, but the clinical notes mention "ataxia, muscle weakness and unspecified lack of coordination." Ataxia is the medical term for the diminished coordination of her right hand. Also, at about this time, she was becoming slower to process conversation when multiple people were present. PSP was sneaking up on her. It's easy to look back now and see what was happening, but at the time, in real time as all this was happening, we didn't know what to think.

On December 13, having seen the neuropsychologist and gone to multiple physical therapy sessions, we finally saw a neurologist, Dr. Howard Kirshner. Dr. Kirshner is an old family friend. Dr. Kirshner went asked her to perform a series of coordination movements. First, he asked her to touch her finger to her nose. She did fine with her left hand, but she missed with her right. He then asked her to tap her fingers together. Again, she struggled with her right hand.

We would do touching and tapping every time we saw a neurologist. It seems to be a favorite neurologist ice breaker. I can only assume they use the same strategy at cocktail parties, business dinners, and dates to kick off conversation—touch and tap, touch and tap. The touching and tapping exercise led Dr. Kirshner to order a new MRI. Again, nothing untoward showed. Dr. Kirshner felt he needed more information to make a diagnosis. He showed us on the scan that the left lobe of the putamen was not as big as the right lobe. The putamen processes dopamine. Dopamine is a neurotransmitter, the deficiency of which causes restless legs syndrome (RLS), which I will get to shortly. It is also associated with the more common parkinsonism, Parkinson's disease. He also said that the left side of the putamen is associated with movement disorders on the right side of the body, possibly accounting for Kay's dexterity issues with her right side. Her symptoms—ataxia, slurred speech, balance issues—made it clear to Dr. Kirshner that something was amiss, but the scans were showing nothing definitive. He said he would like his colleague Dr. Tom Davis, a movement disorders specialist, to see Kay.

After Christmas, we were able to see Dr. Davis. One of the frustrations of the last four years has been the hurry up and wait aspect of the process. We saw Dr. Green in July following her fall. We had been seeing physical therapists all through the fall. Almost six months later we were still seeing doctors and living in this world of ambiguity. We thought we might get a diagnosis from Dr. Kirshner in December, but then he sent us to Dr. Davis. But Dr. Davis couldn't figure it out either. Each appointment with a doctor was an anticipatory event. Each time we thought we would get a diagnosis, but each time it was just touch and tap, touch and tap. We felt so helpless, all the while knowing something was wrong, but not knowing what.

I remember two distinct moments in our trips to the Neurology Clinic at Vanderbilt. The first was the initial appointment with Dr. Kirshner when he said that from looking at the MRI, it was not a brain tumor. All along, I had been silently fearing a brain tumor, a cancerous, malignant brain tumor. I almost burst into tears with relief when I heard his words. I guess I thought the worst was now behind us. I did not know what "worst" could really mean.

The second moment occurred as we were leaving Dr. Davis's office after one of our visits and ran into Dr. Kirshner. We exchanged pleasantries for a moment, and Dr. Davis offered that he was still puzzled. Then Dr. Kirshner said that he really thought it could be corticobasal degeneration. He didn't offer it as a diagnosis, but threw it out as a possibility. As previously noted, corticobasal degeneration (CBD) is an atypical parkinsonism, like PSP. I went home and googled CBD. I was steeled for some life-altering diagnosis, like Parkinson's disease or a brain tumor that we could treat and live with. I had not come to grips with an atypical parkinsonism diagnosis that could have far worse consequences. I was arrested by the information that I found on the internet.

Kay, ever strong, took it in stride. She did not come home and do the research that I was doing. At least, I don't think she did. It doesn't matter. I don't think she would have processed Dr. Kirshner's observation any differently even if she had done the research. She was that strong. We were going down a rabbit hole, one small step at a time. Just like the fabled frog in a vat of warming water, we were slowly coming to a boil.

Dr. Davis told us that the best way to determine whether she had Parkinson's disease was for her to take carbidopa-levodopa, the generic name for Sinemet, for three weeks. Usually, a Parkinson's disease patient will see immediate relief. She got no relief. We saw Dr. Davis again on March 8 after following his instructions relating to the carbidopa-levodopa dosages. This time he ordered a DAT scan, which she had on March 21. Now that CBD was on the radar, we were anxious about the DAT scan, but it was inconclusive. In an email message to Kay, Dr. Davis said the DAT scan "showed a decrease in dopamine transporter binding" consistent with Parkinson's disease and CBD, but he said that he and his colleagues thought a PET scan could be more helpful. What did all that mean?

Each time we saw Dr. Davis, her balance would be slightly worse than before. He suggested that we see a physical therapist named Colleen who works with Parkinson's disease patients. Since most Parkinson's patients have trouble with balance, she uses boxing as a therapy to enhance balance. So, in early 2018, Kay started going to boxing classes twice weekly. She continued with Colleen even after her diagnosis, which came later in 2018. And then, when she could no longer stand on her feet to box, Kay continued on with Colleen, using other strength and conditioning therapies. She worked hard to maintain her strength and health with Colleen until therapy became physically impossible.

At our March 8 appointment, we discussed a second opinion with Dr. Davis. We suggested Mayo Clinic, not because we had any specific, verifiable knowledge of Mayo Clinic, but just because of its reputation. In late March, before the PET scan, we raised the possibility with him again. Dr. Davis was receptive to the idea and said Mayo at the Rochester campus would be a great place to go. He said Kay's case was complicated, and he would welcome a second opinion. We went to the website and made the appointment ourselves. It was relatively easy. Dr. Davis had to make the referral after we talked with a nurse there, which he did promptly. By the time we saw Dr. Davis again on April 10, we had the appointment.

Throughout all these doctor visits, occupational therapy visits, X-rays, boxing lessons and MRIs, Kay was a true champion. She did all the therapies with good cheer. She practiced at home. She was dutiful.

With dogged perseverance, she made every effort to beat this thing, get on top of it. Looking back now, it is so sad. She never had a chance. Maybe she knew she didn't have a chance. She always had a sixth sense. Throughout our marriage, she could frequently read my mind, sometimes with deleterious consequences for me. She claimed special powers. She believed in ghosts. Maybe she really did have special powers. Maybe, she knew before I knew. Maybe she knew my fears before I could verbalize them.

Whatever she knew and was not saying, she kept going to appointments and doing her best. It was in her DNA. She could do no less. Someone with whom I talked, who had been on this journey with a loved one, told me after Kay had been diagnosed that I shouldn't even see the doctors and therapists anymore. They could do nothing. That person was right, but I kept taking her and she kept going. Those visits gave us something to hold onto, look forward to, and anticipate.

As we moved into 2018 and her balance was getting worse, we could still get out and go places. We went to Rosemary a few times. We were having dinners with friends. We went to Chicago for a long weekend with friends to see the Broadway play *Hamilton*. We took the entire family to Legoland in Carlsbad, California, for spring break where Kay, in her indefatigable, daring style, rode a backwards roller coaster with her grandchildren. I didn't ride the backwards roller coaster. Kay even organized a seventieth birthday party for me at Topgolf and invited all my buddies and their wives. She never wanted to stop going and doing and giving.

5

Restless Legs Syndrome

Snakes crawling in my legs

Perhaps it is here where I should pause and talk about restless legs syndrome, or RLS. All her adult life, Kay had suffered from RLS. As previously noted, it is caused by a dopamine deficiency in the body. It can be a terrible disease in its own right, albeit nonfatal, and many people have it in varying degrees of severity. I can't imagine the sensation that it causes. Kay would describe an episode of RLS as feeling like "snakes crawling in my legs." As I perceived the sensation, it was not pain, but an unrelenting sensation of needing to move. Kay experienced these episodes more frequently at night and anytime when she was in a prone position. RLS victims, not surprisingly, also suffer from sleep deprivation. Kay spent many sleep-deprived nights over her adult life. Maybe RLS is why she accomplished so much in her lifetime. Many nights she would be up all night, and when she was up, she was always doing something. Even in the daytime, she could never be still.

RLS started in earnest when we were first married. I was not the cause. I want to be clear about that. It was pure coincidence. It was at its worst when she was pregnant. It is genetic. Her mother had it. Her siblings have it, and two of our three children have it, but I don't think anyone in the family has or had a case as severe as Kay's. It seems to occur more frequently in women than in men. Doctors know that it is caused by the malfunction of the putamen, but they don't know why. It is treatable with a variety of dopamine agonists, or dopamine substitutes, all of which she had taken at one time or another in her life. RLS becomes a major player in this story as we move along.

I have described and will describe further the symptoms and consequences of PSP, but keep in mind that while this insidious disease was wreaking havoc in her brain and body, her legs were giving her fits. When her legs were acting up, she could not sit still. She generally didn't have trouble with her legs in the mornings. Usually around two o'clock in the afternoon, she would start having trouble. Nights could be brutal.

Sometimes the discomfort Kay felt was not apparent to anyone around her, while other times her legs would jump visibly and uncontrollably. Occasionally, she would grimace as the sensation set in, and she tried to control it. Walking helped relieve the sensation. Standing helped. When she could still walk, she would get out of bed at night and pace the bedroom floor back and forth. As her balance got worse, she would sit on the side of the bed, moving and kicking her legs, but usually she would want to get out of bed and walk. Eventually, she could not walk unassisted. At that point, I needed to walk with her. There were many nights when we just walked and walked in the middle of the night.

Heat seemed to help in her struggle with RLS. For years, she would take an extremely hot shower at night immediately before going to bed. She endured water at scalding temperatures just to settle her legs down. She was like a Middle Ages ascetic torturing herself, but the hot showers seemed to help. In the winter, when she could neither sleep nor walk without help, we would go to the living room and stand by the fireplace for an hour or two. The heat of the fireplace seemed to help. Many nights, neither of us got much sleep. There would be periods when it was a lot better, and then it would come back again.

Early in 2018, we changed her restless legs doctor to Art Walters, a neurologist at Vanderbilt, who was reputed to be one of the best RLS doctors in the country. We first saw him on January 30, 2018, and had a pretty constant conversation with him, either in his office or via the Vanderbilt patient portal or by phone (we even had his cell phone number) over the ensuing years as her legs worsened.

Her previous RLS doctor had prescribed a patch that secretes a dopamine agonist, called rotigotine, into the body. She was using the patch when she started seeing Dr. Walters, but it was not enough to calm her legs. He increased the dosage in the patch and started experimenting with other medications and combinations of medications. I think Dr. Walters almost gave up in exasperation. Finally, during one of our visits, he said that some people get relief with a combination of Advil and Tylenol. He was already prescribing gabapentin, a pain medication. He eventually added a small dosage of methadone and a nighttime dosage of clonazepam. She eventually was taking all of these.

As we searched to find the right drug or drug combination, we turned to our longtime and trusted friends Yvonne and Gordon. Gordon is a distinguished, world-renowned pulmonologist and critical care doctor at Vanderbilt. Yvonne is a nurse practitioner in the pediatric intensive care unit at Vanderbilt Children's Hospital. In discussions with Gordon about the medications, he helped us understand the advantages and dangers of the medications prescribed by Dr. Walters, and we started experimenting with the dosages and timing of the medications on our own.

Since she did not have restless legs in the morning, we started administering the medications in the afternoon, with the exception of gabapentin, which is a slower-acting drug than the others that she took morning, noon, and night. Finally, we hit upon a cocktail of drugs administered at 2:00 p.m., 6:00 p.m., and bedtime. We called it the Gordon Cocktail. She started to get better.

Dr. Walters served us well, but having someone with whom we could talk friend-to-friend at any time allowed us to find the dosages and timing that were right for Kay. The Gordon Cocktail was not a magic elixir, but it was an enormous help and became her constant drug regime for the rest of her life. RLS did not go away, but she started to sleep better and have a much better quality of life.

Once again, I counted our blessings. We were fortunate to have brilliant medical professionals a cell phone call away. All the way through our struggle with both these diseases, I thought often about how hard it must be for people who do not have the relationships and resources that we had. Our journey was incredibly hard, but we had a lot of advantages. We were blessed in that way.

6

Diagnosis

Why is this happening to me?

Rochester, Minnesota, is a lovely place in the summer. We arrived on June 4, 2018. Having left the oppressive heat and humidity of Nashville for this southern Minnesota hamlet, we enjoyed delightful dinners at outdoor cafes, attended a summer music festival, and soaked up the culture of another place. It would have been a wonderful short vacation, except for the serious business we had to attend to. Rochester is home to Mayo Clinic. If there ever was a company town in the fullest sense of the phrase, Rochester has to be it. Mayo seems to permeate every aspect of life in Rochester.

Mayo Clinic is set up for people like us who come from a distance and have to make the most of their time when they are there. We'd been assigned a neurologist before our arrival, and our first stop was a consultation with that neurologist, Dr. Jeremy Cutsforth-Gregory. He immediately cut through our apprehension with his quiet personal manner. We felt that we were in good hands. Dr. Cutsforth-Gregory explained to us the battery of tests that Kay would undergo over the ensuing four days and the purpose for each test. We'd brought with us all the scans from Vanderbilt. He studied those, but he said that he would like to do his own scans as well. He explained that in addition to the scans, she would have some other tests as well, with interesting names like the tilt test and sweat test.

Mayo Clinic runs like clockwork. Everything is arranged when you arrive. Everyone knows what everyone else is doing. We stayed in a hotel on campus and walked to all Kay's tests and scans from the hotel via underground tunnels. These tunnels were extremely helpful when we returned to southern Minnesota in February for a follow-up visit.

The purpose of much of the testing was to determine whether she had PSP or multiple system atrophy (MSA), another atypical parkinsonism. I am not totally sure what difference it made, as both diseases are fatal and untreatable. The symptoms are much the same, and we found out in the February follow-up visit that both PSP and MSA are tau related and lie on a continuum, so that a person can have some indications of both. MSA tends to be asymmetric in its effects on the body; that is, it affects one side of the body more than the other. Asymmetry was present in Kay's symptoms, but other MSA indicators were not. For instance, MSA patients tend to act out their dreams in their sleep. Kay did not do that.

At the end of our four days, we saw Dr. Cutsforth-Gregory again. When we left the hotel to go see him for the last time, Kay knew and I knew—the message was not going to be good. We saw the doctor. He confirmed that she had PSP. Kay took it with her normal aplomb. There was no drama, just probing and questioning. I tried to remember as much as I could from what Dr. Cutsforth-Gregory said, and even asked him if I could record the conversation. He explained that her balance and dexterity issues came from degeneration in the midbrain and cerebellum, those parts of the brain that lie at the spinal stem and are the most fundamental and primitive areas of the brain. He said the inability to express thoughts was coming from the tau protein clumping on the transmitters that move thoughts and actions around the brain. Remember, dopamine is such a transmitter. There are others as well. Degeneration of these transmitters is one of PSP's traits that distinguishes it from Parkinson's disease. Although Parkinson's is also a degenerative brain disease, it is focally centered. PSP and its cousins are more generalized in their attack on the brain and produce very different consequences.

Thinking back on that day, Dr. Cutsforth-Gregory said two things that stood out to me and remain with me even now. He said the disease will eventually take your life. He said it in just that way. He didn't use words like "die" or "death" or "terminal." They are shocking words. They are words that, for whatever reason, he chose not to use. Instead, he said the disease will "eventually" take your life. Maybe he thought saying it that way would make it easier for us. Maybe he thought that particular turn of phrase would make it easier for him.

The other thing Dr. Cutsforth-Gregory said, I assume as a way to reassure us, was that his diagnosis and the presence of this disease did not signal an imminent end of life. He said that it could be ten years before she would even need a wheelchair. He was right about the disease taking her life, but he grossly overstated the time before a wheelchair would be needed. Eighteen months after we saw him, she needed a wheelchair. Ten years later, she would have been dead for over six years. Maybe that is what he meant when he said she would not need a wheelchair.

We returned to the hotel room. We had a plane to catch, bags to fetch, and a drive to the Minneapolis airport ahead of us. I don't know how much we processed things, but finally, she broke down and sobbed. She just sobbed uncontrollably for five or ten minutes. While she sobbed, she said, "Why is this happening to me?" It was a question she would ask, and I would ask, countless times over the next three years. We went home to confront our future. She didn't cry again for the rest of the trip.

7

Driving

Don't it always seem to go that you don't know what you've got 'til it's gone

"Big Yellow Taxi"—Joni Mitchell

The day when Kay lost the privilege to drive was one of the most devastating moments in our journey. For the most part, our lives did not change after we arrived home from Rochester and resumed living day to day. We didn't want our lives to change. We were moving on, knowing that hard times were ahead, but wringing all the joy we could out of the time we had left.

She continued to drive after we returned home, going and coming on her own schedule and continuing to bask in the independence that she still enjoyed. Then, one day late in the fall of 2018, she came home and told me that someone had rammed into her car while it was parked in the parking lot of the Green Hills Mall. She said she came back to her parked car to find the front bumper and grill smashed without even so much as a note from whomever had hit the car. By now, I had adopted a philosophy of not worrying about anything that did not involve life, death, or bankruptcy. I told her it wasn't a problem and not to worry about it. I reported the damage to the insurance company and made arrangements to get the damage fixed.

A few days later, she came to me and told me she had lied. That was her term—"lied." In fact, she was pulling into a parking place at the mall when she hit the accelerator instead of the brake and rammed the car in front of her. Instead of being hit, she had been the hitter. Further, she left without leaving any information for the driver of the damaged car. She had never hidden the truth from me in all our married years, she had seldom used the word lie in any context, and she had never manufactured a fictional tale as elaborate as the one she had related initially. Moreover, to have damaged anything belonging to someone else without offering to fix it, to make it right, was totally out of character for her. She was desperate. She was scared. She never drove again.

We knew her coordination wasn't good enough for her to drive and be safe for herself and others. So she voluntarily stopped driving and depended on me to take her to places she needed or wanted to go. But she still had her license. She could still drive if need be. All of our generation had lived for that day when we could have a driver's license and enjoy the independence that goes with it. It was and continues to be one of our dearest possessions. She still had her license even though she never planned to drive again.

In the fall of 2018, we were seeing Dr. Green with some frequency, and soon after the accident we saw her again. This time Dr. Green brought up the subject of driving. She "suggested" that Kay be evaluated at the Pi Beta Phi Institute by a therapist who has a specialty in evaluating people's ability to drive. I don't know whether doctors are required to refer someone they suspect of impaired ability for evaluation, but I think Dr. Green knew that she should refer Kay and knew what the outcome was likely to be. Kay went without objection. She took a written test on our first visit and went back a second time to take a driving test. I took her both times to Pi Beta Phi and waited while this nice young woman administered the tests. The driving test was a real driving test in our car on actual streets. I know Kay must have been nervous and scared. It must have been demeaning to be behind the wheel trying to convince this young woman a third of her age that she could drive and drive safely. We immediately received the evaluation verbally after the driving test ended. The therapist told Kay she could not drive again and she would have to surrender her license. She said that she was compelled by law to report her evaluation to the Tennessee Division of Motor Vehicles.

That day, February 15, 2019, was one of Kay's worst days. It was one of my worst days. It was heartbreaking. She knew she shouldn't be driving and had voluntarily stopped driving, but she still had her license. She had earned that license when she was sixteen years old. Now it was being taken away from her—and along with it, her independence. She was no longer fully herself. She was someone different from everyone else, and someone headed down the road to an agonizing death. And she knew it. And she cried. And I cried with her.

We left for Australia the next day to visit our daughter and her family. When we returned, waiting for her was a steely cold letter from the Division of Motor Vehicles, unsympathetically titled "Notice of Proposed Susp. Medical." Then she had to suffer the indignity of signing a letter with her faltering hand, addressed to the DMV, and enclosing her surrendered license never to be issued in her name again.

Life with PSP--The First Year

I can't do anything

By Christmas of 2018, soon after the accident in the mall parking lot, she was clearly getting worse. On December 22, we had dinner with all of Kay's siblings and their spouses at the home of her brother Tom and his wife, Cathy. The evening was lovely, just the kind of evening she normally enjoyed, punctuated by good food, good cheer, and the pleasure of being with her family. When we arrived home, I asked her if she had a good time. She said not really. She said the night was really hard for her. She was having trouble following conversations, forming her thoughts, and participating.

The next night, we went to a dirty Santa party. The party had become an annual event with two other extended families, including the in-laws of our daughter Jennifer. The party had grown every year as additional babies were added to the mix. She looked forward to the event each year and the prankish delight of coming up with funny presents that no one could possibly want to receive. On this night, she mostly stayed in one place the whole evening and had very little to say.

We were invited to a number of other holiday parties and retirement parties throughout the month of December. We even made a brief appearance at a second Christmas party the evening of the dirty Santa party. She went to all of them, but her demeanor each time was the same—quiet and reserved.

Kay and I were at home all day on Christmas Eve 2018 until four o'clock services at church. We were still trying to live a normal life. I was focusing on a project in the bedroom, while she was attempting to put bows on Christmas presents in the dining room. After a short time, she came to me professing, sadly, that she couldn't put the bows on the presents. She was frustrated and upset. She said through tears, "I can't do anything." I helped her finish with the presents, and we had a few laughs at my ineptitude.

After we finished the presents, she asked if I thought she was getting worse. I said no. Then I asked her what she thought. She said she thought she was. I asked her why. She again referenced the evening at Tom and Cathy's family party. She said the dirty Santa party was hard too. I asked her why. She said it just takes so much effort to talk and she doesn't have anything to say. I hugged her, and she cried really hard for a few minutes. I had observed for some time that group events, like cocktail parties, were hard for her. In those settings, the conversations go fast, back and forth, and overlap each other. She just could not do that anymore. The cocktail party, the dinner party, any social event had always been her milieu. Sadly, it was no more.

As time moved on, it became increasingly difficult for her to participate in groups of more than two or three. As the disease progressed, she was bathed in the love and attention of good friends, but it was becoming difficult for her to participate in group chats. Even with one-on-one or two-on-one conversations, I had to caution people to let Kay talk. She could not form her thoughts fast enough to engage in even these more intimate conversations. She might have something to say, but she had to be given time to say it.

Personality change and aphasia, the inability to generate speech, were very early signs of the disease. So, too, was difficulty with her eyes and her sight. I learned from researching PSP and from our visit at Mayo that difficulty with the eyes is a classic symptom of PSP. The term "supranuclear" in the name PSP refers to the inability to control the up-and-down movement of the eyes. Falls are a constant danger for PSP patients. We were told at Mayo many of the falls that assail PSP patients are caused by the inability of a PSP sufferer to have the peripheral vision necessary to see walking surfaces, leading to trips and falls. I never observed her having trouble moving her eyes up and down, but maybe loss of peripheral vision had something to do with the fall she took in 2016 while pushing the grandchildren in the stroller.

Whatever difficulty confronted her in the movement of her eyes, other difficulties with her eyes were constantly present. She seemed to suffer from light sensitivity continuously. Sometimes she complained of blurriness or double vision. Maybe tunnel vision was a part of it. She was never able to articulate the problem well enough for those of us around her to really understand what she was seeing.

I first became aware of how light sensitive her eyes had become when, in early August of 2018, we went with our friends Mike and Trisha to Russia. For as long as I can remember, she had wanted to go to St. Petersburg and see the Hermitage. I was determined that we were going to do it while her health was still strong enough for her to enjoy it. When we were finally there and touring these glorious galleries inside the Hermitage, seeing treasures that she had longed to see, she wore sunglasses throughout the day. I kept saying to her that she should take them off, that she was missing all the beauty. She refused. She wanted to be there. She wanted to see all that was there, but she couldn't stand to let too much light into her eyes.

Even the slightest sliver of light was a problem for her. We had a big flat-screen TV in our bedroom. Strapped to the back of the TV were two boxes, one a cable box and the other an Apple TV box. The cable box had a small light that indicated it was receiving power. Switching off the lights in the bedroom at night enhanced the glow coming from the cable box's power light. Every night I would have to cover the TV with a blanket or towel to hide the power light's glow. Later, she became obsessed with wearing an eye mask for sleeping. For months, she slept with a mask. It was like a security blanket for her. Then, for no discernible reason, she stopped wearing it.

Our house has a lot of natural light, but there are areas where artificial light is needed even in the daytime. She always requested that we dim the lights. She wore sunglasses many days inside, and as her condition worsened in years two and three, she kept her eyes closed a lot.

The night after Christmas 2018, our entire family, with grandchildren, convened at our house. It was fun and chaotic, and she seemed to enjoy the night. Afterward, I asked her if she had a good time. She said she had trouble seeing. She said that she had double vision. That night was the first time that I recall her complaining of her eyesight in that way. As mentioned earlier, the cataract surgery did not produce the results that she'd anticipated, but she had not previously complained of double vision.

Early in the progression of the disease, she lost the ability to read a book or newspaper. She said she couldn't focus her eyes well enough to pick out the words on the page and couldn't move her eyes side to side well enough to follow the lines across the page. She did not lose her eyesight. She could still see, but she could not read.

After Christmas, we went to Rosemary Beach. We were having dinner together there, just the two of us, when she asked me whether she should know more about the contents of the CurePSP.org website. I had pored over that site, taking in all the dour consequences of the disease, but she had never looked at it. She wanted to know if she should learn more about the disease. I told her the website didn't say anything that she had not already heard when we were at Mayo. In fact, it contained significantly more information than she had been exposed to, but I didn't want her knowing all that was ahead of her. She had been content to take the disease a day at a time. That was her coping mechanism and it had been working. Why add more anxiety to the anxiety she was already silently feeling? The next day, she asked again, so we read it together. She saw the prediction in the site of the years a patient survives until the disease takes the patient's life. She saw other bad news as well.

She was uncharacteristically quiet for the next couple of days. I think she was processing what she had learned and confronting the harsh fact that she was unlikely to live as long as Dr. Cutsforth-Gregory had led her to believe. She had always known that the disease would take her life, but I think the website made it more real and immediate.

While we were in Rosemary Beach, Jennifer and Lauren's families joined us. During our stay, there was a lot of conversation about Lauren's in-laws, Patty and Brian, joining Lauren's family after Kay and I left. Lauren and Brian were moving to Australia soon after the Rosemary Beach trip, so this would be a goodbye visit for Patty and Brian. By the time we left, despite all the discussion, she did not remember any of those conversations. She was becoming more disoriented.

In January 2019, she was still walking pretty well, but she was having terrible restless legs spasms. We still had not gotten her medications right. She was using the rotigotine patch and had begun taking gabapentin, but nothing seemed to work. All through January and February, the jumpy leg problem persisted. There were nights when she didn't get to sleep until three or four in the morning. When she would get out of bed to pace, I would sometimes get out of bed and help her walk. When she was just sitting on the side of the bed kicking her legs or seemed pretty stable on her feet, she would tell me to go back to sleep. The nights when I would doze off and leave her alone, she might be pacing or sitting on the side of the bed by herself for hours. What goes through your mind when you know you are dying, you can't sleep, your legs are incorrigible, and you are alone in the dark with your thoughts?

Through this period, she was going to the bathroom at night often, both further interrupting her sleep and creating the risk of a fall. On one particular night, January 28, 2019, she got up to go to the bathroom by herself and fell backward in the shower. She was not hurt, but it was a foreshadowing of what was to come.

About this time, I began to notice all of her symptoms becoming more pronounced. Her ability to communicate was getting worse, not so much the slurring of words, but more difficulty in forming thoughts.

Also, her right hand was getting more stiff and unusable. Her fingers on that hand were starting to curl into a claw-like fist. She was eating exclusively with her left hand. She was losing her ability to even approximate the touch-and-tap exercise, particularly with her right hand.

Despite all that was going on, we had a lovely Valentine's evening in 2019. She wanted to live life to the fullest, and that meant enjoying our evening together. Her ability to put the disease in its own little box, out of the way and out of mind, continued to astound me. We had the day to ourselves, just the two of us. It was very nice, despite the fact that the next day was the day she had to take the driving test that resulted in the loss of her license. She was taking one day at a time without thinking about what the next day might bring; or perhaps thinking about it but keeping it all bottled up inside, safely tucked away.

Lauren and her family moved to Sydney, Australia, in late January of 2019. They anticipated being away for at least two years. Both Lauren and Brian, knowing that Kay's decline would be ongoing while they were away, agonized over the decision to move. I assured both of them they were doing the right thing. Brian's work needed him in Australia more and more, thus requiring frequent long-distance travel that took him away from the family. Our lives would go on, we could come and visit soon, and Lauren could come home periodically to see her mom. They needed to be together as a family. Kay agreed wholeheartedly. But for both of us, losing Lauren's daily presence in our lives was a major emotional loss we had to confront and manage.

A trip to Australia had always been on our bucket list. With Lauren and family now there, we had an excuse to go, and we thought Kay's health would allow her to make the trip. I knew, however, that the window for us going would close soon. Waiting until Lauren and Brian were settled and familiar with their new surroundings before becoming our hosts would have been optimal. But I knew that we might never go if we did not go soon.

We had our second appointment at Mayo Clinic on February 20–22, and immediately left for Australia afterward for a three-week visit. We bought a business class ticket for Kay so she could stretch her legs and stand up when the inevitable RLS spasms started. I sat in premium economy to make it all financially feasible. I didn't like being separated from her for plenty of reasons, but mostly I worried about falls. Defying my worries, she made it without incident.

The trip was a big success. We spent a lot of time with the grandkids. We saw Lauren and Brian's new house. And, of course, we saw one of the most beautiful cities in the world. Kay could still walk well enough that we could do daily explorations as long as I held her hand and steadied her. One day, Lauren dropped us in the Paddington neighborhood south of the city center, and we walked over six miles through Paddington toward downtown that day, ending our journey at the ferry stop in the middle of the city. We held hands the whole way, and she did great.

We were sitting in a gelato place in Sydney on March 3 when I asked her if she was feeling okay. We had been on a boat all morning, and I was concerned she might be a bit queasy, having always suffered from motion sickness. She said she was not feeling motion sick, but that she did not feel well. She said she never feels well anymore. She worries about what other people think when she doesn't talk. She said it is just really hard to talk. I asked her whether it was hard because it was hard to physically move her mouth and face to form words and make sounds, or hard because she could not form her thoughts. She said it was both. She said that she just didn't have anything to say.

Her self-analysis was right on target. I was noticing that her aphasia was getting worse. She wasn't talking unless asked a direct question to which she was compelled to respond. True to her personality and singular regard for the feelings of others, I think her concern with aphasia was not her declining health, but a concern that other people would feel disrespected or dismissed by her. As time went along, I would say to people in her presence that if Kay was not talking, it wasn't due to lack of interest or engagement. I think doing that helped her.

On March 8, we were still in Sydney. That night was the first night that she wanted me to help her get to the bathroom. She had fallen the previous night and cut her ear.

Earlier that night, we'd been to the opera with Brian and Lauren at the Sydney Opera House preceded by dinner at an elegant restaurant in the city. She was excited about the evening and did well throughout the dinner. She also seemed to do well during the opera, but she later said she was having trouble seeing the surtitles. As is the usual custom with opera houses, surtitles displayed above the stage help the audience understand the dialogue. I asked her if she could see the stage clearly or whether her double vision bothered her. She said she could see the stage, but she couldn't see the surtitles because she couldn't lift her head enough to see them. I have already addressed the classic PSP symptoms of inability to move the eyes up and down. Perhaps her difficulty in seeing the surtitles was not a matter of lifting her head, but a matter of lifting her eyes.

Her regard for others throughout this ordeal was remarkable. She sat without complaint throughout the evening in one of the most spectacular venues in the world watching an opera without the benefit of the surtitles necessary to follow the plot line, just as she had worn sunglasses at the Hermitage without complaint. She made no complaints to Lauren, Brian, or me, nor did she say a word about being unable to see the surtitles until we were alone back at Lauren and Brian's house. That's the way she was. She didn't want to ruin someone else's evening with her complaints.

On one of our days in Sydney, we went with Lauren, Brian, and the grandchildren to an amusement park. We all decided to ride the bumper cars. Kay, as unsteady as she was, was still up for a thrill however she could find it. She and Anna, her seven-year-old granddaughter, paired up in a car. Somehow, in the bumping, her hand got caught between her car and another car, and she broke her finger. The incident was not a consequence of the disease, but it was one more malady with which she had to deal.

We returned to Nashville in late March. We had splinted her bumper-car finger, but when we returned home, we went to a walk-in clinic to get an X-ray. The X-ray confirmed that the finger was broken, but the doctor said there was nothing more to do than put it in a splint. I would say that the thrill of the ride and her time with Anna was well worth a broken bone and whatever pain and discomfort came with it. We were going to see a lot of splints, slings, and braces in the weeks and months ahead.

Easter that year occurred on April 21. We were invited to Easter brunch at the home of Jennifer's brother-in-law and his family. All of our family was included, except of course Lauren and Brian, who were still in Australia. That day stands out for me as a turning point in the journey with PSP. Even though her balance and ability to walk had deteriorated somewhat while we were away, she seemed noticeably less steady on her feet Easter Sunday. In the preceding days, she had become more labored in her speech and more reticent to speak. On that day, among these people who were her family and extended family, she was sadly withdrawn and quiet.

By Easter of 2019, we had become accustomed to worsening symptoms followed by plateaus followed by declines. The declines were slight at first, but the overall trajectory was downward. Easter of 2019 is significant because the decline in her condition was more dramatic on that day and the days leading up to it.

Two days later, April 23, we engaged Val Reese as Kay's daytime caregiver. Engaging Val was a spectacularly fortuitous decision. Kay's condition was such that she could not be alone anymore. Even with someone with her, she was subject to frequent falls. At first, Val came in the mornings four days a week. Eventually, we expanded her hours so that for most of the time throughout the rest of Kay's life, she would come each weekday morning at seven thirty and stay until three in the afternoon. Later we were able to find additional help, but for months, Val and I were the only caregivers. She was with Kay during the weekday daytime hours, and I was with her for the rest of the time. That's the way we did it.

In the spring of 2019, falls were becoming a major problem. Dr. Cutsforth-Gregory had told us one of the great dangers of PSP and the reason many people lose their lives to it is the propensity of PSP patients to fall, break a hip, and never recover. Further, for some reason people with PSP are prone to fall backward, creating conditions ripe for broken wrists and arms. Kay did fall backward on occasion, but she also found multiple other ways to fall. She was still convinced that she could walk and stand. Because walking and standing is instinctual in all of us, adapting to the loss of balance and the ability to walk takes some adjustment. As she adjusted and we adjusted, we went through a significant fall phase. Further, just as she did not want to surrender the independence conferred by a driver's license, she did not want to surrender the independence of walking and standing. She had to be watched carefully lest she place more trust in her body than it could handle.

Very soon after we hired Val, Kay fell and broke her wrist. Val was not with her that day. I was. I am sure Val and I let her walk more than we should have during the spring and summer of 2019, and without question, Kay tried to walk more than she should have. The result was the first of many broken bones.

At some point during that first week of Val's employment, while she was still assessing how to handle Kay and Kay was still convinced she could walk, Kay fell into and broke the big picture window in our bedroom. At another point during this phase, when she could still walk, but not very well, Val was getting her on the commode in the powder room of our house when Kay fell against the commode's water tank. The porcelain tank cracked open. It would have taken quite a force to break the tank. I find it remarkable that a woman who was five feet three and weighed no more than 125 pounds could deliver a force sufficient to break a porcelain water tank.

We'd now entered the orthopedist phase of the disease. We had been referred to Dr. Paul Rummo when Kay broke her finger, and by the time the falls became a problem, we already had a relationship with him. I think over the next six months or so, we probably put his first-born through college. We had a follow-up visit with Dr. Rummo for her finger the day after she broke her wrist, a fortuitous convergence of events allowing us to double dip a finger and a wrist. Now she had a splinted finger and a cast on her wrist.

Prior to our Australian trip, she had been seeing Colleen twice a week to work on boxing and balance. When she returned from Australia with her broken finger, she continued with Colleen despite the bad finger, further evidence of her tenacity and determination not to let PSP take control of her. When she broke her wrist, boxing had to cease. Undaunted, she went back to Colleen after her fractures healed to do weight training and muscle toning.

For me, one of the really pitiful and sorrowful things about this disease was that she kept trying to self-improve. She did everything that anyone told her to do to take care of her body. She never stopped taking the calcium pills and women's multivitamins that she had taken for years until the late stages of the disease when she could no longer swallow well enough to continue. At night, when I would get her in bed, she would have me apply a cream to her face to keep her skin healthy. When she would fall and scrape or hurt herself leaving a break in the skin, she would have me apply Vicks BabyRub to the damaged area because she said it would prevent scarring. She never gave up living even though she knew that none of our efforts would extend her life or slow the progression of the disease. Even highly paid, rigorously trained professional athletes do not have the kind of tenacity and determination that she had.

We had another appointment with Dr. Kirshner, the neurologist, on the same day that we saw Dr. Rummo for her finger and wrist. That was the first step in getting the RLS problem under control. Dr. Walters, the RLS doctor, after initially prescribing methadone as a medication for RLS, told us, after she had taken it with success for several months, that he could no longer prescribe it because departmental policy required that every prescription of an opioid must be done through the pain center at Vanderbilt. We then went to the pain center, where a Dr. Edwards, who seemed like a perfectly competent and good physician but who seemed to know nothing of Kay's total medical situation, said she had to cease taking methadone. What a disaster!

She came off the methadone dosages gradually, but when she ceased taking them, her RLS became the worst it had ever been. She couldn't sleep at all at night. I couldn't sleep. We were up most nights just walking, with me holding her so she wouldn't fall. All this was occurring at a time when death and addiction to painkillers was becoming epidemic nationwide. The State of Tennessee was trying to get the situation under control, and all legitimate providers were doing everything in their power to help. Nevertheless, Kay was dying and withholding the medication that seemed to be helping the most seemed inhumane. We found out later that her dosage was so low she would not have become addicted in any event.

Through our struggles with PSP and RLS, I went through many fits of anger and frustration with doctors, but on the whole, they were doing as much as could be done for the diseases she had. My patience gave way, however, when Dr. Walters and Dr. Edwards refused to keep her on methadone. She was suffering. She and I were exhausted. I was enraged. I understood the rationale, but the rationale did not apply to a terminally ill woman in agony. That month without methadone was one of our worst. I was miserable. She was even more miserable. We explained all this to Dr. Kirshner, and he readily agreed to prescribe it. We gave thanks at the shrine of Howard Kirshner many nights after that.

She was born on June 15, 1949, making June 15, 2019, her seventieth birthday. Tom and Cathy invited all our family and all her siblings and their families to their house to celebrate. The event of the day was the presentation to Kay of a book of rhyme and drawings, in the vein of a graphic novel, titled *The Terrifically True Tales of Super Kay and How She Always Saves the Day*. Barton had come up with the idea and had written the script while Jennifer, Lauren, Kay's sister Pat, and unofficial family member Caitlin curated the art from friends, grandchildren, and themselves. Caitlin had managed production. It was a portrait of Kay, her life, and her personality done in fun, whimsical color. Barton had the honor of presenting it to her. He read the book to her while her four-year-old granddaughter Scout sat in her lap. The book came as a total surprise to both Kay and me. It was one of those really magical moments that our family will always remember. She was delighted and overwhelmed. It could not have been a more satisfying day.

Even that day, her special day, a day of unbridled joy and escape, was marred by a fall. We left her unattended momentarily. I think a child had bolted toward the pool, and the attention of all in attendance turned in that direction, leaving Kay alone. She stood and tried to go to a window to see what was happening and went down. Fortunately, she was not injured, but the fall snapped us all back from the glory of the day to the reality of her life and our lives. All throughout this period, her impulse was to walk and stand. She thought she could still do it. She was unwilling to admit that she couldn't.

It had been a year since her diagnosis.

9

Life with PSP--The Second Year

I did it!

Over the weekend of June 22 and 23, 2019, Kay and I traveled to St. Louis with friends to see two major league baseball games. Kay was able to walk from the hotel to the game, navigate the ballpark concourses and seating, and enjoy the outing. Everything went smoothly without incident until we retired to the hotel room for the night. She was sitting on the side of the bed as I brushed my teeth and prepared to join her when she decided she needed something from the side table next to the bed. Rather than asking me to get it for her, she reached over and fell into the side table, breaking two ribs. The trip was fun and provided a great diversion for both of us. It gave us the opportunity to fill our lives with as much happiness as we could glean from our circumstance. But it ended with another trip to Dr. Rummo.

We went to Rosemary Beach again over the July Fourth weekend. This time we flew. She gladly accepted a wheelchair in the airport. Her pride was breaking down. She didn't want to be seen by anyone, stranger or friend, in a wheelchair, but she was beginning to have no choice.

After we returned from Rosemary, she fell again and broke her shoulder. Once again, we were visiting with Dr. Rummo. With all these fractures, she seemed obsessed by the pain. She was not one to submit to or complain about pain, so it is worthy of mention that Kay kept complaining of pain long after it should have disappeared. The wrist and shoulder particularly gave her a lot of problems. She would complain of the pain and insist that we go back to Dr. Rummo. We would go. He would examine the wrist or shoulder and say it was healing just fine, and then, a couple of weeks later, we would do it all again.

Sometime in the summer, Dr. Green, in an effort to help her with her speech, referred her to an otolaryngologist, Dr. Kimberly Vinson, at the Vanderbilt Voice Center. We saw her on July 18. As we walked down the hallway to the office of Dr. Vinson, I began to understand that her clientele was seeing her for much different reasons than Kay was seeing her, for on either side of the hallway were pictures of the who's who of country and pop singing stars. I guess I should not have been surprised given Vanderbilt's location in the middle of Music City, USA. Frankly, I didn't care who had been there before us, I just wanted Kay to be able to talk.

Dr. Vinson's technical support staff put a camera through Kay's nose into her throat so the doctor could look at her vocal cords. After viewing Kay's vocal cords, Dr. Vinson explained that they were stiffening, like other muscles in her body, such as her hands, her arms and her legs. In order for Kay to talk, she had to exert an enormous amount of effort to push enough air through her vocal cords to make a sound. She recommended more physical therapy at Pi Beta Phi Institute, this time with a voice specialist.

Back at Pi Beta Phi, we met Kelly, our new voice therapist. Kelly had done her homework. She seemed to understand PSP and its effects on the voice. Early in our time with her, she made clear to us that Kay was going to reach a point at which she would not be able to talk at all and that putting her through a battery of voice exercises was going to be fruitless. She became something of a villain to me and to Kay's sister-in-law Cathy, who had trained in her younger years as a speech therapist. I think Kelly cared deeply for Kay, but she just happened to be the messenger bearing a message that was difficult for us to hear.

Kelly concentrated her attention and Kay's efforts on a voice-generation computer manufactured by Control Bionics that was designed to talk for a patient when the patient could not talk for herself. The Control Bionics technology consists of a computer screen with letters, words, and phrases, and a bracelet worn on the patient's arm. By focusing the eyes on the letters, words, and phrases and slightly moving a hand or finger while wearing the bracelet, the patient can command the computer to generate a voice that speaks the selected words and phrases. Kelly even had Kay record her own labored voice so it could be used after Kay completely lost her ability to speak.

We saw Kelly weekly throughout the fall and early winter of 2019 as she tried to train Kay to use the device. As amazing as the device was, Kay could never focus her eyes well enough to activate it. A lot of thought and effort went into preparing Kay to be able to use the Control Bionics technology. The vendor for the technology even had a sales representative come to our house on multiple occasions to try to find a way for Kay to talk using the technology. It was a total loss, not for lack of trying, the good will or the technical sophistication of Control Bionics, or the good intentions of the therapist. All the equipment landed in our basement, and after Kay died, I returned it to Pi Beta Phi hoping someone else could use it.

We discovered that similar voice generation technology was available on her iPad by downloading the appropriate app. We tried to use the app by having her touch words and phrases on the iPad screen. She was never able to tap. She didn't have enough dexterity in her hands to do anything more than lay her finger on the screen, and she didn't have enough control of her eyes to find the letters, words, and phrases to be tapped. The disease won again.

Throughout 2019, Kay's speech became softer. It seemed harder for her to talk at all. When it was just the two of us, she would just sort of grunt out yes or no or commands such as needing to go to the bathroom. Even when Kelly tried to record her voice at Pi Beta Phi, the effort needed for Kay to project enough for the recording to work was gargantuan. Val was better at understanding her than I was. She would say to Kay, "Take a deep breath, Kay, and force it out." Kay would do it, and we could understand her most of the time, but it took great effort.

In July of 2019, she was still able to travel. The Crystal Bridges Museum of American Art in Bentonville, Arkansas, was on her list of places to see. So, in July, we drove with our friends Doug and Sondra to Little Rock, Arkansas, spent the night in a lovely hotel there, and drove the next day to Bentonville. We stayed two nights there and then flew home. Again, as in the airport the previous month, she was willing to accept a wheelchair at the museum. Even as tenacious as she was, she knew that she couldn't walk the expanses of the art museum. We had lunches and dinners in restaurants each day of the trip and stayed in a lovely Victorian bed and breakfast. Even on this wonderful trip with friends, she could not escape restless legs. Her legs wouldn't let her sleep any night that we were away. We had rooms all three nights that were large enough for her to pace the floor sufficiently to relieve some of the discomfort, and that's exactly what we did for a major part of each of those nights.

No matter how she tried to pursue pleasure to escape PSP and RLS, she could never get totally away. But she did not, would not, permit those diseases to ruin the life that she had left. Notwithstanding the encroachment of her disabilities, I think she truly loved the trip to Bentonville, just as she had loved the trips to Russia and Australia and the sojourns in Florida. She had an extraordinary ability to block out the unpleasantness of her health and focus entirely on the joys of the moment. Those times when she could still go places and do things were precious times for both of us, times not to be wasted.

It was not long after our return from Crystal Bridges that walking became untenable. Her balance continued to deteriorate, and now she was also dragging her right foot so that sometimes she walked with a shuffle. It was no longer sufficient just to steady her by holding her hand. She had to be held up and helped in order to walk at all.

Her cognition was also slipping in the late summer and fall of 2019. She was becoming more easily confused, although memory and base knowledge were unaffected. She could tell you in detail where some item of clothing or cookware could be found in the house or where some file folder was lodged, but processing current information was getting harder. At night, presumably because she was tired, she was pretty out of it, almost catatonic at times. She would know what was happening, what she needed to do—like brush her teeth or get to the commode—but she seemed unable to relate knowing with doing.

She was getting tough to care for. She was strong willed, obsessive, and determined. We had not yet acquired a wheelchair, so she still sat in regular chairs. She would sit for a while and then want to get up and do something or see something or just walk. She continuously alternated between sitting and standing dozens of times a day. All that up and down and moving around was exhausting to a caregiver. All this was made worse by her inability to sleep at night. On those nights when she didn't sleep well, which came in abundance, she would be in a daze the next day. She refused to lie down and take a nap or just lie down and rest. I don't know whether it was the RLS or just personality, but she could not sit or be in one place long enough to rest her body.

On August 9, she received a letter from Clark Lea, at that time the defensive coordinator on the coaching staff of the University of Notre Dame football team, and now, as I write, the head coach of the Vanderbilt University football team. Clark spent a large part of his high school years hanging out with our son, Barton, and their buddies in our basement. Kay was the den mother. She took care of all those boys, and they loved her. She had known Clark since he was in fifth grade. His letter was personal, sweet, beautifully written, and totally unexpected. When I read it to her, she broke into tears and cried out, "Why is this happening to me?"

In late summer, we acquired a walker, hoping that it would give her some independence. We purchased one with wheels and hand brakes, thinking that a walker without wheels would require some lifting and would contribute to backward falls. Unfortunately, she could never use the walker because she couldn't use the hand brakes, and the wheels made it likely the walker would get out from under her and contribute to more falls. The walker thus became one more medical device that she could not use.

Despite growing impairments wrought by PSP, her impishness, particularly when friends were around, never abated. She was always intent on being the consummate hostess and entertaining her friends. One day in early September, three or four women came to see her not long after our purchase of the walker. She was quite proud of it and wanted to show off her new toy to her visiting friends. She was in the living room and started with her walker toward the front door, which is surrounded by big floor-to-ceiling windows. When she attempted to turn around and come back toward her audience, she lost her balance, lost control of the walker, fell into one of the floor-to-ceiling windows, and broke the window. She did not fall through the double-paned window nor did it shatter, but it did have to be replaced. Remarkably, she was not hurt. We had seen Dr. Rummo enough.

On September 8, we went to church for the first time in a long time. She did surprisingly well, and there were many well-wishers. We even went to a downtown bakery with a fellow parishioner after church. We didn't take the walker, but by then we had a push wheelchair we could use. Then, Sunday night, her legs started to physically jerk and jump as they sometimes did. It was a particularly bad episode, and she did not sleep well that night. Monday night was much the same. The same thing happened late in the day and into the night on Tuesday. The jumps came about every ten seconds. I could time them almost to the second. After that episode, her walking deteriorated. She started dragging her right foot more. Sometimes, her right leg would completely give way. It was as if her gait just fell off a cliff that week of September 8. For the first time, she was willing to consider buying a motorized wheelchair.

Each year on the first weekend in October, the International Storytelling Festival is held in the town of Jonesborough, Tennessee. Kay had been on the board of directors of the Storytelling Center for a number of years. We had been going to the festival each year since she had been on the board and for a few years even before she joined the board. It had become something of a tradition for us. Once again, as testimony to her unwillingness to surrender her life to this disease, she insisted on going. We went with our friends Doug and Sondra. There were no falls and no fractures. We took the push wheelchair with us, and she rode in it the whole time. She was becoming more comfortable being out and about in a wheelchair.

By mid-November, her PSP symptoms seemed to have plateaued. She had not gotten worse in any respect other than a noticeable decline in her stamina. In early November, we took a ride in the country to seek out a farm we'd owned and enjoyed earlier in our lives. That evening, we attended an engagement party for a child of one of our close friends, and then, that same night, we went to a wedding reception for the child of other close friends. The two days it took Kay to recover proved to both of us that even though she had plateaued, she had her limits.

Despite her condition, December 2019 had its high points. I think anyone facing a disease such as this has to remember there are good times, precious times of great intensity that could never be replicated. In the fall of 2019, knowing that death was looming and that further decline was inevitable, Kay decided she wanted to have a dressy, festive holiday cocktail party for all her friends and family. Lauren and her family were coming home from Australia for the month of December. Kay bought a new dress for the party, which was planned for some 150 people on December 15. On the night of the party, her sisters, Pat and Susan, did her hair and makeup and got her dressed. She looked herself—beautiful, radiant, and joyful. Knowing that Kay couldn't stand throughout the evening, Susan bought a tall director's chair in which Kay could sit and be at eye level with her guests. A receiving line of sorts formed around the chair, with each guest bending over and putting their ears next to Kay's mouth to hear what she was trying to say. Taking on the persona of a queen receiving her court, she conversed with all of them. The pictures from that night show a supremely happy woman surrounded by the people she loved and who loved her.

The other major event of that Christmas also found its origin in the fall of 2019. Kay read, or had read to her, an article in the *New York Times* about a young mother who had terminal ovarian cancer. This young mother hit on the idea of doing a legacy book so that her children, who would grow up without her, would always know something of their mother. Kay decided that she wanted to do something similar. So, she recruited Val to help her and began collecting pictures of our family. She also included pictures of her parents and some of her ancestors. She and Val made three bound Snapfish books of pictures, with some input from me, one for each of our children, with each book focused primarily on that child. Without my knowledge, she made one for me as well. She also dictated to Val a letter for each of the children and one for me, expressing her love for each of us. Then, she had Val place each letter in the front of the appropriate book. She also included in each book a passage that she liked from *The Library Book* by Susan Orlean about not being forgotten. The books are and forever will be another testament not only to Kay's love for her family but also to her determination to create something remarkable and immortal even as she was under attack from PSP and RLS.

The books were printed and prepared in time for Christmas. On the morning of Christmas Eve, we invited the three children and their spouses to our house for a special surprise presentation. They knew nothing about the books. It was a total surprise. That morning was probably the high point of her whole struggle with the disease. It may have been one of the happiest days of her life.

On February 17, 2020, we went to the Belcourt Theater, an art theater in Nashville, to see *Parasite*, the film that eventually won the Academy Award for Best Picture that year. We didn't know in advance that the movie was a foreign language film with subtitles. Of course,

Kay couldn't read the subtitles, so we left and came home. We found the movie on one of the streaming channels, and I read the subtitles to her as the movie played.

In early 2020, she was having more trouble moving her legs, especially her right leg. Getting her in and out of the shower and in and out of the car were becoming more difficult because she couldn't help as much as she had helped previously.

A gait belt was suggested to us. Over the course of several months, we found ourselves with several gait belts. Like the Control Bionics computer and the walker, we could never use any of them. The gait belts are designed for someone who is unsteady on her feet but can walk. These belts didn't work for Kay, as she had to be physically supported in order to walk.

COVID-19 hit in March of 2020, and stay-at-home orders were issued. Although we'd been staying at home most of the time anyway, we were receiving many visits from friends. Those visits stopped, at least for a while. Thankfully, Val continued to come despite the risk, but I feared that the lessening of contact with other people would hasten Kay's decline. She was certainly getting worse. At dinner, she could barely hold her head up. We usually watched a movie at night, but now she couldn't hold her head up for the entire movie. It would just drop down on her chest.

On March 24, we watched one of our favorite shows—*This is Us*. At that time, the episodes came out once each week on Tuesday. We would eagerly await the new episode and watch it the night it was released. On this night, she couldn't remember watching the last episode the previous week. She would have these periods when she seemed to be in cognitive decline. That same night, we argued about the day of the week. She insisted it was Friday. Finally, I found enough hard evidence to convince her it was Tuesday. I suppose forgetting what day it was during a pandemic lockdown was excusable, but it worried me that her cognitive abilities were declining.

RLS can come in waves and then subside. She had enjoyed a respite from RLS in the early spring of 2020, but in April the discomfort came back with a vengeance. She could not sleep at night. When she would have a leg episode, she would wear down quickly. She didn't have the stamina to bear up under the onslaught of RLS. This went on incessantly for days and then it subsided again. On many occasions, I have puzzled over how much the ravages of RLS hastened the progression of PSP and eventually her demise. We will never know.

Easter Sunday in 2020 was April 12. Again her legs were jumping. Jennifer's family came over despite the quarantine. We had other visitors. We FaceTimed with Karen and Rob, college friends who now live in Cincinnati. You might remember that Karen was the erstwhile matchmaker in college who brought Kay and me together. We FaceTimed with other friends. Her sister Pat and her husband, Bobby, defied the quarantine and had dinner with us. For an Easter in the middle of a pandemic, it was not bad. She seemed to enjoy it all, but all the activity and the battle that she was waging with her legs exhausted her. Her stamina was on the decline.

In the fall of 2019, Kay had been fitted for a motorized wheelchair that had the potential to give her a higher level of independence than she had enjoyed in the past. The wheelchair, a Quantum iLevel, had to be specially made and fitted for her. It was an expensive and sophisticated piece of equipment, but we found that Medicare would pay 80 percent of the cost, making it accessible to us. We had been anxiously awaiting its arrival for months. Finally, in April 2020 it was delivered. The chair was unwieldily, weighing in excess of 400 pounds, but the structure and seating were designed to allow her to sit in it for hours at a time without causing her skin to break down as might have been the case with a less well-built chair. In addition, it had a joystick for directional control, multiple positions that allowed her to sit however was comfortable to her, a lift that would raise her to eye level of someone standing next to her, and multiple speed settings. We had great hopes for the chair's utility when it arrived. Without question, the chair improved her life. She spent most of the rest of her life in that chair, but it did not provide the level of independence that we had sought. Sadly, she didn't have enough control of her hands to manage the joystick or any of the other controls. The technician who delivered it even installed the joystick on her left side so it would be accessible to her good hand, but it never worked. We had to drive and operate the chair for her. It became just one more piece of sophisticated medical equipment that she could not fully use.

Kay's inability to operate the wheelchair controls never stopped her from trying. By the end of her life, she had dented our refrigerator, knocked a hole in the kitchen wall, damaged baseboards throughout the house, and relocated our marble-topped 150-pound dining room table, all by ramming the wheelchair into whatever was in her way. Having the wheelchair required even more supervision of Kay because unsupervised, she would grab the joystick and run over something or someone.

On Sunday, April 19, Kay said when she awoke that she did not feel well. "I do not feel like myself." She said her legs were stiff and hard to move. She tried to walk, but she couldn't move her legs well enough to do so. Then, in the midst of "not feeling well," she decided she wanted to walk on the treadmill.

At the time, we had a treadmill in the playroom in the basement. Getting there involved going out of the house to external stairs. She could barely walk. How was she going to descend and ascend stairs? I tried never to say no to her throughout all of this ordeal, so I said, "Let's give it a try."

She labored mightily to make her way down and up the steps. I was holding her to keep her from falling forward going down and from falling backward coming up. She had to summon enough energy not only to make her legs move but also to lift them on the ascent. As we slowly descended the stairs, one harrowing, difficult step at a time, the outcome was by no means clear. I feared for her safety even with me holding her, and I feared she might collapse at any moment. When she walked the last step and reached ground level, she blurted out with her impaired voice in a clinched-fist way, "I did it!" That was one of her high moments. It was one of mine too.

Somehow, with my help, she managed to get herself from the stairs, across the sizable playroom to the treadmill, and then get on it. She walked five minutes on the treadmill with me holding her to prevent a fall. After she'd exhausted herself on the treadmill, we had to climb up the steps she had just descended with so much effort. The fact that we made it is just one more remarkable moment in her battle with PSP.

How can any of us understand what it is like, how frustrating it is, how depressing it is to be as debilitated as she was? How could this otherwise robust woman be in this shape? When most of us become temporarily ill or impaired, we can look forward to getting better over days or months. Kay, though, could only anticipate getting worse. What must that have been like? The little victories counted. She needed a win. She got it. She had won a small victory over PSP. I love to think of that moment when she exclaimed, "I did it!" She was still a competitor, a winner.

On Friday, May 15, she and Val went to her friend Judy's house and had lunch around Judy's pool. It was a good day, but for the first time she said that swallowing water made her cough. Swallowing is a typical PSP problem and can lead to aspiration and pneumonia. It scared me. However, it was more than a year later, when she became very sick, before swallowing became an issue.

I have spoken only in passing of personality changes. One of the threads that ran through the disease was obsessiveness. Those who knew Kay might say that obsessiveness was a thread that ran through her whole life. But, that obsessiveness was about getting the job done, achieving a goal, helping people. This obsessiveness was just the inability to let go of anything lodged in her mind.

She became obsessed with TV shows. One of her favorites was *The Morning Show*, a TV serial drama that premiered on November 1, 2019. She watched that show over and over. She must have watched each episode five or six times. Poor Val had to watch with her in the afternoon, day after day, and I had to watch with her at night. The other shows she watched all the time were *This is Us*, *The Voice*, *Jeopardy*, and *Big Little Lies*. At one time or another on the journey, she was obsessed with all of them.

In the early stages of the disease, we began to write the story of our life together. Every afternoon when Val left, Kay and I would go to the room in the house we called the office, where my laptop normally resided, and write down our experiences together. The therapist I was seeing occasionally suggested this activity might be rewarding to both of us.

At first, she could still talk and it was fun. She would talk and I would type. We laughed a lot and dredged up old memories. As time went along, she lost most of her ability to talk, but she was still obsessed with continuing to work on it. It became more of a chore than a diversion for me, but she would not quit until the labor of talking became too much, and she gave it up. It is now a treasure of forty-four single-spaced pages that I need to finish for all posterity. Like many other achievements in our lives, I owe a lot to her obsessiveness and relentless determination.

Another obsession was the board game Rummikub. She wanted to play it all the time. She would make Val play with her. She wanted to play every night when Pat and Bobby were with us for dinner. She was never very good at it. The game involves matching tiles on the playing table. She did pretty well with it in the early days of 2020, but by September, she was having more trouble with her eyes and complained that everything was blurry. I think there was a cognitive challenge as well. As more tiles were displayed on the board, she couldn't keep them all straight. She eventually reached a stage where she couldn't keep up with the tiles well enough to play at all. Thus, one more chapter came to a close.

The first weekend of June, Rob and Karen, our friends from Cincinnati, came to spend the weekend. Kay loved being with those two, particularly Rob. A fun guy with lots of stories, he could make Kay laugh by just walking in the door. They arrived on Friday afternoon, and Kay wanted to stay up late to be with them that night. She was fighting RLS. She was exhausted, but did not want to give up and go to bed. We finally excused ourselves to start the bedtime routine. She took her shower as usual, but I couldn't get her out of the shower. She couldn't move her legs and feet. I finally managed to get her up and out of the shower chair, but I couldn't get her any farther. Then, she went limp and I couldn't hold her up. She collapsed to the floor. Now we were both on the floor just outside the shower. I tried several times to lift her by her arms by putting my hands or forearms through her armpits, but her arms had no life in them and would flop up from her shoulders. I tried everything I could think of and nothing worked. I considered calling Karen and Rob to help. But she was sitting there naked, and I was mostly naked from being in the shower bathing her. I didn't want to call them in to view this sad spectacle. Finally, in one mighty heave, I was able to get her up. She was exhausted, and I was exhausted. The same thing happened once or twice later. It was scary when it would happen because I couldn't do anything with her. She became a 125-pound ragdoll.

By now, her stamina had been declining over several weeks. She would even take an occasional nap. She was coming very close to being unable to speak. She could mouth yes and no and maybe bathroom, but we were mostly reading lips and hand signals. Her right arm had gotten much more stiff and uncontrollable. Most of the time, it would clutch up next to her side or trail out behind her, which made getting her dressed more difficult. She would spend a lot of time sitting slumped over in her chair.

It had been two years since diagnosis.

Life With PSP--The Third Year

We need to prepare for my demise

In early July, Lissa, our priest for pastoral care at the church, came to see Kay. She has a talent for conveying love and compassion, but she does not shy away from talking about death and dying and God's love in the face of all that death entails. Kay cried some. She seldom cried. After Lissa left, she said, "I just want to be normal." It was in those moments that we could not deny the disease. Those moments when something was said or something happened that brought the disease into full relief were heartbreaking for her and for me.

Later in the month of July, for some reason we went to the mall, maybe to just get out of the house. As we left the house, she paused and asked for her clutch purse that held her credit cards and her ID. She so much wanted to be normal, to be herself. That little clutch purse gave her identity, maybe even hope. It was important to her that she have it with her. For me, it was sad to see her grasping at life.

Sometime in July, I did not date the entry, I entered two quotes from her in my journal. She could barely talk by this time, and I could barely understand her, but I think she said, actually I am certain that she said, "We need to prepare for my demise." And she said, "I just feel empty and alone." So sad. We both felt alone. But how much worse it must have been for her. She was almost totally locked in—unable to stand, walk, read, write, or talk. Without communication with other people, no matter how many friends come to see you, you cannot relate, be intimate, converse. How alone she must have felt!

By mid-year 2020, she was sitting with her head on her chest more and more. Her head would just get lower and lower, always tilting to the right side. We had several suggestions for back braces to keep her upright. We bought and tried several because she looked so uncomfortable. Like the other medical devices we'd tried, none of the back braces really helped. In one of the late stages of the disease, much later than mid-year 2020, I asked her if it was more comfortable wearing one of the braces and sitting up straighter or more comfortable slumping forward. She indicated as best she could that it was more comfortable to slump.

In September 2020, I bought a Honda conversion van with an automated ramp that extended from the side of the van. The ramp allowed us to roll the big Quantum iLevel wheelchair up into the van and position it where the front passenger seat would normally go. Getting her into our SUV had become almost impossible. Even if I could get her seated in the SUV, she would sit slumped over against the door. With the van, she could stay in her wheelchair and ride more comfortably. The van was a welcome addition and enabled her to be much more mobile.

I rented a golf cart. The dealer let me try it out for a month. I thought it would be a nice substitute for long walks. Metro Nashville Parks has a golf cart for people with disabilities that can be taken into Warner Parks near our home. I had taken her into the park a few times, and she had gone with her friend Elizabeth a few times. I thought having a golf cart to use in the neighborhood on pretty fall days would be something that she would enjoy, but it, like so many other efforts at ameliorating the burden, did not work out. She would slump over and almost fall out. Even strapped in, she felt insecure, so we gave up on the golf cart after the one-month trial.

In addition to the medical equipment already mentioned, we had a variety of other medical equipment. I installed toilet safety rails early in the life of the disease. As it became more difficult to get her in bed, I bought something called the Etac Turner Pro, which was essentially a platform for standing that rests on a swivel so that the patient can stand on the platform and be turned. It did not adapt well to the bathroom space, but I could use it to get her from her wheelchair to our bed. Of course, after a while she could no longer stand well enough to use it.

We were given a pedal machine that allowed her to pedal and move her legs while sitting in a chair in hopes that it would help her legs without her having to stand. It did help for a while, but eventually she was unable to use it anymore. We had three wheelchairs—one that we pushed, an inexpensive motorized wheelchair that we purchased to bridge the gap to the big Quantum iLevel chair, and the big boy itself. We had socks to keep her feet warm and compression hose to address RLS. We tried everything we knew to try and everything anyone suggested.

In mid-October, we were watching TV. At the end of the episode, for some reason, I felt moved to say to her that I am so sorry that this is happening to you and so sorry that you have to endure this. I told her that I try to be upbeat, but really I am sad all the time. I told her that it hurts to see her suffer. She seemed touched and a little emotional. I said I am sad because I love you, and I don't want bad things to happen to you. That night, as I was getting her into bed, she said that she did not want me to ever say those things to her again. I asked why not. I told her that I just wanted her to know how much I cared. She said not to say those things again because it made her feel bad. She said this is the way I am now. She said she was going to be this way for a long time.

In a conversation the next day, at least what passed for conversation, she said that I should want to divorce her. I said no. I said that we are in this together. I said I will always be here. I didn't know what to make of her comments at first, then I began to think that maybe she didn't want to be reminded how difficult her situation was for both of us. Taking into account Kay's pride in self and her own identity, she may have interpreted my comments as pity for her. Even though she said not to talk as I had the previous night, the next day, she was very clingy with me and wanted my presence more than usual.

October 19 was a tough night. At about five in the afternoon, she shut down. She said, "You don't know what it's like to sit all the time." She was crying and seemed really depressed. Our good friends Doug and Sondra had dinner with us that night, and Kay barely acknowledged them. Putting her to bed was a real challenge. She was limp all over. I couldn't get her to brush her teeth. She just stood slumped over with the toothbrush in her mouth. I finally took it away. I feared she was going to hurt herself. I didn't know whether she would be able to get her pills down. She did, but only because I held the cup of water to her lips and pulled her head back for her to drink. She was getting more and more slumped over. I asked her if it would be okay for me to try and straighten her up occasionally. She said no. It was better to be slumped.

The first week of November, her legs started jumping again. She was really having a hard time feeding herself. She had been eating with her left hand for a long time, which never worked particularly well, but she could sort of get it done. By the first of November, she was reaching the point where she could not do it, but she was adamant about not allowing someone else to feed her.

On November 30, our friends George and Ophelia came to visit. They came almost every Friday afternoon at three o'clock sharp. Kay enjoyed their visits, but on this day, she hung her head the whole time they were with us. The previous day, our longtime friend Susan came to visit and read to Kay. It was nine thirty in the morning, but Kay went to sleep as Susan read to her. The previous night, she was so tired I could barely get her in bed. As each day would go along, she would decline visibly. She would sit with her bottom lip out and her head bowed.

For many months, she had been drooling. She would sit with her mouth gaped open with moisture dripping out. She often carried a pretty handkerchief with her, and we always had a cloth napkin at hand. We got in the habit of always using cloth napkins for everyone in attendance at dinners because that's what Kay used. We had medication for the drooling, but it never really curtailed the flow very well. Strangely enough, when she entered her final days, the drooling stopped almost completely.

On December 1, she was sleeping more. She stayed in bed most of that day. Val said that she thought Kay might either be depressed or bored. Maybe she was just tired. She went back to bed three times that day and canceled a visit from her friend Judy after having slept nine hours the previous night.

We were having some work done in Rosemary Beach, and I was going down for one night to check on it. She got emotional about me going. She said, "I wish I was dead."

Despite these low moments, she always had something she looked forward to. In the fall of 2020, Val and I, with Kay's oversight, planted daffodils in front of the house across the driveway where the windows of the dining room look out on our beautiful lawn. She wanted the daffodils planted where she could see them. She was thinking of spring and the beauty of spring flowers. What she did day-to-day most of the time, even to the very end, was consistent with living, not dying.

By mid- to late-January of 2021, she was getting more and more tired, with hardly any stamina left after the noon hour. At night, it would sometimes take as long as a half hour to brush her teeth. It was also becoming apparent that she couldn't control her mouth and tongue well enough to move her food from her teeth to her throat so that she could swallow the food. As I would brush her teeth, I would find packs of food in the side of her mouth. Some, or all of it, would wind up in her jaw, making it necessary to put my finger in her mouth and dig it out. There was no alternative. Some nights, I would skip the shower and put her straight to bed. I was afraid that she'd be so unresponsive that I wouldn't be able to get her out of the shower.

On January 24, the kids were with us, Barton and his family in the afternoon and Jennifer and her family at night. Kay went to bed really early. She seemed depressed. Perhaps being with the family without being able to interact with the grandkids depressed her. She'd also soiled herself while Barton was with her. I had to clean it and her up. That probably depressed her too. That night she wet the bed and the next day she urinated in the wheelchair. We had been able to keep the incontinence under control for most of the time in the last year, but she went through a period in early 2021 when it became worse.

Before we moved to our current house, we lived on Richland Avenue in another part of town. Our next-door neighbors there were Linda and Richard. Linda had been in poor health for a long time, and was now at the point of death. Kay wanted to go see her, so we did. Getting her in the house to see Linda, who was semicomatose with only a few days to live, had its difficulties, but we were able to do it. She sat for a long time holding Linda's hand, these two beautiful ladies near the end of their lives, probably fully aware of their own mortality sitting quietly with each other. There Kay was with only a few months to live visiting her dying friend, doing God's work.

In January of 2021, Nikki Johnson started as Kay's nighttime care-giver. She was quite good and by late spring, Kay was adjusting to her. By then, her difficulty eating had increased, and I would feed her while I ate. She did not want anyone else to feed her. I tried to get her to accept Nikki, but she refused. As time went along and May rolled around, she tentatively allowed Nikki to give her food. I was especially concerned that she wasn't getting enough nutrition. Val and I were doing all we could do, aided by Nikki in the evenings, to get vitamins and protein into her. We started giving her Ensure and Carnation Instant Breakfast to supplement the morning protein-laced fruit smoothie that had been her daily fare for some time. I told her that she had to start eating more, that I was getting concerned. After that, she really tried to eat.

When we got hospice involved in January 2021, I started getting more information from the nurse and social worker who came to see her each week. I learned from them that, as she neared death, her body was probably telling her not to eat and that the food probably didn't taste good to her. For many weeks, she subsisted on milkshakes, ice cream, and baked potatoes. Soon she grew tired of them as well. She never lost her desire for sweets. The hospice nurse said the taste buds that detect sweets are the last to go. I guess it is comforting to know that when our time comes, we will always find pleasure in a Reese's Peanut Butter Cup.

As May dragged on, she became more agitated and restless. She would have a look on her face like she was in pain. I don't think she was feeling pain. If asked whether she was in pain, she would shake her head, no. I think she just felt bad. It was becoming a little more frequent that she would wet herself while sitting in the wheelchair. Of course, that was upsetting when it would happen.

By mid-May she showed no interest in going out or doing anything. Her friend Elizabeth liked to get her out of the house. Val was also good about getting her out. She just didn't want to go anymore. Sometimes she would have a blank faraway look in her eyes, especially in the mornings. She was sleeping more and more, both in her chair and in bed. I think she was also becoming more disoriented. One evening when it was just the two of us, Lauren called from Sydney. Lauren and I talked and tried our best to include Kay in the exchange. That's how all conversations went at this stage. A little later, after the call ended, she seemed to ask me, "Where is Lauren?" I could have misunderstood what she was saying, but it seemed as if she thought Lauren was somewhere in the house.

May 29 was our fiftieth wedding anniversary. Since Lauren was still in Australia, we delayed our official celebration until July when she and her family could be with us. In lieu of a formal celebration, I invited any and all Kay's friends to eulogize her in advance, that is, tell her then how much she meant to them and how much they loved her. Funerals, memorial services and burial offices are wonderful for the living, but what do they do for the dead? Rather than waiting until Kay was no longer with us to tell her all those things that are said at visitation and those services, how about telling her now while she could still comprehend and appreciate what was being said?

A steady stream of people flowed through the house all day on that beautiful spring day. Our friend Judy made a wedding cake. People gave her cards and remembrances. I read them to her one at a time. Rob and Karen came down from Cincinnati. I gave her a pair of expensive earrings and read to her a long love note that I had written.

The day could not have been better. I think she enjoyed all the attention and felt the love. It was hard to tell. She was usually welcoming to visitors and tried to do what she could to make them feel at home. It was striking when she was unable to do that. But despite her diminished ability to show emotion in her usual way, on this day, she seemed herself and seemed happy.

It had been three years since her diagnosis.

11

The End

Beyond the door there's peace, I'm sure
and I know there'll be no more tears in heaven

"Tears in Heaven"—Eric Clapton

Lauren and her family arrived back in the United States on July 1, 2021. Because of the COVID pandemic, they had not been back to the US since December of 2019. It had been eighteen months since Kay had seen them, and she was looking forward to their return. It was a grand, joyous day. The hospice people said we might see her condition deteriorate noticeably after Lauren came home because she would have expended so much emotion and energy in anticipation of that day that she might not have anything left. The hospice staff had been saying for some time that they didn't think she would last long. Actually, they didn't think she would even live to see Lauren's family's return. She'd continually proved them wrong, and she did it again.

Our formal wedding anniversary was celebrated on July 17. We held the event at Lauren and Brian's new house. It was a lovely day and a beautiful event. The best man from our wedding, along with one of the other groomsmen, and their wives traveled to Nashville to be with us. Two of Kay's good friends from our military days also traveled to be with us. Gordon and Yvonne were there. All of Kay's siblings, their spouses, and all our immediate family were there. There were speeches and tributes. I think it was very meaningful to Kay. Once again, we expected a steep decline in her condition after the celebration, but it didn't happen. She was too tough, too resilient, too determined.

What did happen after the July 17 celebration, though, was an even sharper decline in her speech. We had been lip reading for several months, but now we couldn't even do that. She was left with only two ways to communicate. She would raise her left hand when I walked by her wheelchair, meaning she wanted me to sit down beside her. She also used the raised hand to welcome visitors and let them know she would love their presence by her side. Her other communication tool was to use her left hand to shove me away, and sometimes others as well, meaning she was displeased in some way with the person being shoved. I may have gotten the shove more than others. She never lost her pluck.

Kay spent her days sitting in her wheelchair at the dining room table, with Val or me beside her. Through much of her confinement to the chair, she and Val would explore the myriad clothing and home furnishing catalogs that flooded our mailbox, sometimes making a purchase. As time passed in 2021, she even lost interest in that. In late afternoons and evenings, she would fade into a nap or a sort of stupor, characterized by a fixed stare or closed eyes, a drooping lower lip, especially on the right side of her face, and a drooling mouth. It was hard to watch.

Notwithstanding her declining condition, she was still aware of activity around her. Sometime during the summer, our daughter Jennifer and her husband, Daniel, decided to buy a new house. She told Kay what they were doing and Kay lit up. She also brightened when the grandchildren came around. Toward the end, I think the only real joy she had was seeing her grandchildren. She never lost her awareness of people and events, but the only time she was able to show her normal emotion was when the grandchildren were present.

In mid-August, the slope of her decline steepened. She was sleeping longer hours. Sometimes she would sleep around the clock. Her eyes had become sunken. She was barely eating, and getting her to take her RLS medication was becoming more difficult. We struggled to bathe her and put her to bed because she was so limp and unresponsive. She was becoming alarmingly thin.

On the second weekend in September 2021, I went to our house in Florida with two friends just to get away. It had been a year since I had been away from her, except for the one overnight trip to Rosemary in December 2020. Friends and family were urging me to take a break. I was physically and emotionally exhausted even though I could neither recognize nor acknowledge it.

I think I will always regret taking that trip. Kay didn't want me to go, and I knew that she didn't want me to go. Earlier that year, I had promised her we would go to Rosemary together for one last time. I thought long and hard about how to do that—how to get her there, whether she could endure the trip, whether to take Val or Pat with us to help me manage her, how she would feel when she had to say goodbye for the last time to this place she loved? Would the leaving be like dying? I had promised, but I finally decided she was too frail. Then I went without her. I think that really hurt.

The day after our return from Florida, she motioned for Val to leave the bedroom so that she and I could be alone. Of course, she had no way of verbally communicating her feelings, but she found a nonverbal way. After Val left the room, she grasped my face in her left hand and squeezed my cheeks as hard as she could squeeze. Then, she put her hand over my eyes so I could not see her, as if to say "I don't want to see you or you to see me," and then she took her hand away and punched my nose. At the time, I thought I heard her say, "I hate you." When I asked her if she loved me, I think she said no.

I was stunned. At the time, I did not know what to make of her actions, but upon reflection, I think she knew she was in her final days and was saying that now is not the time for you to take a break. She was at her most fragile and insecure state and needed me to be there for her. Not only did she want to maximize her every moment with me, but throughout the illness, I was her one constant, her security blanket. Throughout our marriage, she said that I was her rock. I think that may be why she loved me as much as she did. I could be the rock that allowed her to be impulsive, intuitive, and active. I will always regret that trip. I was her greatest security and her greatest love. She needed me, and I chose not to be there for her.

Soon after the Florida trip, her sister Pat invited me to lunch with her and Bobby. Pat had probably seen more of Kay during her illness than anyone, except for Val and me. But during my Florida trip, she was with her almost constantly. The purpose of the lunch was to register with me her heightened concern that she did not think Kay would last more than a month. Our friend Judy visited us one day during that same week and said the same thing. The hospice nurse and social worker agreed. These were good reality checks. I was never willing, or able, to see the changes in her as readily and with as much clarity as others.

The following week, she was agitated and seemed angry all week. The next week, she seemed sad and depressed. She mostly sat with her eyes glazed over and a faraway look on her face with her mouth gaped open. Throughout the rest of the month, she was eating less and sleeping more. Some days she slept almost twenty-four hours, others eighteen. Occasionally, she would surprise us all and rally and go back to her old schedule and demeanor. It was up and down, but the overall trajectory was down. Her urine took on an orange hue. The hospice people said it's normal for urine to look this way in a person who isn't getting enough fluids. We tried to get more fluids and nutrients in her, but she was becoming less and less interested.

On October 6, a Wednesday, she slept late, which wasn't unusual. Around nine that morning, Val tried to wake her and could not. I tried and was also unsuccessful. I called hospice. The nurse and social worker came right away. Kay was breathing comfortably and showed no sign of pain or distress. They said to let her sleep and showed me the dosages of morphine and Ativan I could use to ease her if she should seem to be in pain or if her breathing became labored or accelerated. We called all our children and her siblings. Her brother Don came from Louisville, and all our kids spent the day at her bedside. Pat and Bobby were there, as well as Tom and Cathy. Later, in the evening, the grandchildren came. Her sister Susan came from Louisville the next day. Lissa, our pastoral care priest from church, came and prayed a prayer that sounded to me like last rites. We were all on death watch, waiting for the end.

All day on the sixth, she was in and out of consciousness. She slept without interruption that night. The next morning she showed more signs of life, but still was not fully awake. Later, in mid-morning, our daughter-in-law, Hayley, brought our granddaughter Tru to the house. Tru, our youngest grandchild, was sixteen months old at the time. She is a pandemic baby, having been born on July 10, 2020. Because of COVID concerns, the pediatrician had cautioned Barton and Hayley to be the only ones to hold Tru for several weeks after she was born. The setting of that boundary had been excruciatingly disappointing for Kay. Barton and Hayley had given their daughter the proper name of Trudy Kay in honor of her two grandmothers. Whether it was because of the pandemic forced separation, Tru being a namesake, or Tru being the baby of the extended family and probably the last of our grandchildren, Kay formed a strong attachment to her. Despite having been semicomatose for over twenty-four hours, when Hayley brought Tru into the room that day, Kay seemed to have an immediate recognition of her presence. When Hayley sat Tru on Kay's stomach, Kay's eyes opened, a smile came to her face, and she started playing with Tru. Tru sat on her stomach for a half hour or so and smiled and cooed at Kay, and Kay smiled and played with Tru. The moment was magical. For the rest of the day, Kay was more alert. Later in the day, we even got her out of bed and into her wheelchair. Tru had literally raised her grandmother from near death. Kay had defied expectations again.

The next day, a Friday, she was better still and rallied to the point that she woke at a normal hour and stayed in her wheelchair all day. She even received visitors the following week and the week after. Then, around October 20, two weeks later, we had a night of labored breathing with groaning sounds. The first night that it happened, I called hospice. A nurse came to the house and advised Ativan and morphine. I administered both. It happened again the next night, and again I gave her Ativan and morphine. Each time it settled her breathing. The next night, she slept through the night without incident and didn't awaken until noon the next day. On the next night, the twenty-fourth, she slept until two in the afternoon. After that, until early November, she usually would awaken later than her normal hour, many days as late as 9:30 or 10:30, but occasionally she would rally and return to her old schedule—up at 7:00, to bed at 10:30 or 11:00.

On Friday morning, November 5, she roused around eight. Val got her dressed and gave her a full glass of smoothie, but she was never fully awake. She sat in her chair and dozed. Finally, Val laid her in bed again, and she slept until two thirty, when Val changed her diaper and left for the day. Kay then slept from the time Val left, all through the night, and all day Saturday until noon on Sunday—forty hours straight. She rallied on Monday and Tuesday, but she was far more nonresponsive than in the past. We managed to get her in her wheelchair, but mostly she sat slumped over. When we asked her if she wanted to lie down, she indicated that she did not. She wanted no part of the bed. She has always been so high energy that beds and naps had been out of the question, so refusing the bed was not a new thing. Maybe she saw the bed as a place where she would die.

Early that week, we had hospice bring a hospital bed so she could stay in bed during the day and sit up. The weekend hospice nurse also recommended giving her oxygen to help her with her breathing. The oxygen arrived on Tuesday. That night she slept in the hospital bed with the oxygen. I didn't like that. I wanted her in bed next me so that I could hold her or hold her hand. We had been sleeping together for over fifty years, and I wasn't about to stop now. I wasn't going to stop until she was no longer of this world. Wednesday night and Thursday night, we slept together.

Each day during this period, her appearance changed from the day before. Each day she became more gaunt and frail. There was almost nothing left of her body. Her eyes receded into their boney sockets. Her cheeks were hollowing out. Her mouth gaped open to get air. She ceased to look like herself. She looked more like a caricature of a skeleton. Early that week, we noticed the skin on her back breaking down. The nighttime caregiver at that time, Keshia, said we should start turning her every two hours. On Thursday, we noticed bad spots on her ankle and heel in addition to the place on her back. She slept most of Thursday, and Keshia turned her that evening when she left for the night.

Keshia told me when she left that I should turn her every two hours over the course of the night. I was possessed by the idea that I had to turn her as Keshia had instructed. I set the alarm for 2:00 a.m. and slept in my clothes so that I would be sure to wake up and turn her.

One after one, family members volunteered to stay with us that night, but I sent them all home. I wanted the night to be as normal as possible. I knew that this was probably her last night. I wanted this night to just be our night. I wanted it to just be us.

I knew what to do if her breathing became labored. I knew that I was supposed to turn her every two hours. I knew I could do all that. I had done almost everything for her for over three years, but for some reason I couldn't turn her that night. I lay awake most of that night feeling guilty that I couldn't do what I was supposed to do. I don't know why I couldn't do it. She seemed so frail and fragile. I was afraid I would hurt her or break her. I just could not do it.

When Kay and I were dating and in the early years of our marriage, her favorite actress was Audrey Hepburn and her favorite movie was *Breakfast at Tiffany's*. I found that movie on Netflix, dismissed all the family, and queued it up. I don't know whether she actually saw any of the movie. It is unlikely. She may have heard some of it. But, I am convinced she knew what we were doing. I am convinced she knew that on this night, the last night of her life, we were watching *Breakfast at Tiffany's*, just the two of us, together, like we did fifty years ago.

Her breathing accelerated that night and became more shallow. I counted forty breaths per minute. In the same way that I couldn't turn her, I couldn't administer the morphine and Ativan. I have no explanation why. I had administered morphine and Ativan in previous nights without a problem. As things developed the next day, turning her became irrelevant, but my hesitancy to administer morphine and Ativan as I had done on previous nights, resulted in her laboring to breathe that night when I could have made it easier for her.

When Val arrived at seven the next morning, November 12, she was still laboring to breathe. We gave her morphine, but the dosage didn't seem to work. I called the hospice nurse around ten, who said to give her another dose of morphine and a dose of Ativan. Her breathing moderated somewhat.

Val and I both thought that we'd lose her this day. Her frailty, her unresponsiveness, and her breathing patterns led us to believe she couldn't last much longer. Our family started to arrive around noon. The hospice nurse and social worker arrived around one o'clock. The nurse thoroughly examined her. She was reluctant to predict anything, but she also thought the end was near.

I, along with Jennifer and Lauren, sat in bed with her with other family members around us in the room. Barton had a meeting that he needed to attend, so he came to be with us and then left for a while for the meeting. After an hour or so of vigil, I decided to lie down for a bit, maybe even take a short nap. Minutes later, Jennifer came to me, saying I should come back to the bedroom, that her breathing had changed to slow breaths. About that time Barton returned, and we all got in bed with her. I held her head on my shoulder and whispered to her, telling her to think of all the good times we had experienced together. I recalled as many as I could think of, saying after each one, "And we were so happy." One of the last things I said to her was that she would be buried at Larkspur Conservation Natural Burial Ground in the place beneath the founding oak as she had requested, and that next spring, we would plant a tree in her honor next to her grave. Then I mentioned the weddings of our three children, what fabulous events they were, and again said how happy we were. Jennifer, Lauren, and Barton said that she drew her last breath as I mentioned the weddings. Yvonne was there with us. It was of inestimable comfort to have a medical professional who was also one of Kay's oldest friends with us that day. Yvonne checked her and confirmed that she was no longer living. I called the hospice nurse and social worker. They came immediately and did their own examination and pronounced her dead. She died at 4:10 p.m. on November 12, 2021, three years and five months from the time she was diagnosed and six and a half years since anyone first noticed symptoms.

Many unexpected emotions washed over me that day. Everyone says I was a wonderful husband and caregiver, but I could only think of all the times when I should have been there for her and was not. I thought of how I could have spent more time with her. She wanted me by her side more than anything, but I just couldn't give as much as she wanted. I had to get away occasionally. I know in my heart that I gave her my all, but once she was gone and there was nothing more that I could do, I started to think of things I could have done, perhaps should have done. This journey took three and a half years out of my life, measuring from the point of diagnosis. But for Kay, it took the last three and a half years of her life. It was a miserable way to spend those years, yet she never wavered in her good humor and resolve. Even in the end, she still wanted to play with her granddaughter. I have a picture of her from early 2020 sitting in her first motorized wheelchair. She is sitting in it as proud as a new Tesla owner. After it was over, the sight of the big Quantum iLevel wheelchair, in which she'd spent so many hours, evoked unbearable sadness. She deserved better—this woman of motion, of doing, of creating—than just sitting in that chair.

There were so many times in the course of this journey when I just wanted it to be over. I didn't want her to die. I just wanted it to be over. This disease had us both imprisoned. I couldn't get out. She couldn't get out. I would think about all the things that I could be doing, would be doing, all the things that we would be doing together. Now it was over, and I was lost. I didn't know, and even as I write this, I don't know what I am going to do. I don't have a plan. I don't have an interest. I just want to be sad. I miss her. I slept alone the night of November 12. I sent everyone home. I just wanted to be sad and lonely. I just wanted to be really sorry for her and for the way she had to live her last years. I pray that she died with peace in her heart.

12

Caregiving

I can't do everything but I'll do anything for you.
I can't do anything except be in love with you

"Romeo and Juliet"— Mark Knopfler

The day it first hit me that I was a caregiver was June 7, 2018, the day Dr. Cutsforth-Gregory at Mayo Clinic gave us Kay's diagnosis. We had known an atypical parkinsonism diagnosis was a strong possibility, but we didn't really know what that meant. She was showing signs of the disease, but our life was pretty normal. She was driving, we were both going about our daily activities much as we had been doing, and we were busy. Being busy helped.

Immediately upon diagnosis, Kay wanted to tell the kids, and then she wanted to tell a bevy of friends. We constructed an email, and she sent it. I am so glad she wanted to be transparent. It made things easier. We didn't have to make excuses for little errant behaviors. It made it easier for her, for me, and for friends. There was no tiptoeing around or pretending that things were normal. It was out there for all to see. She was going to die in the not-too-distant future, and she was going to suffer as yet unidentified disabilities on her way to death. She was also going to wring all the good out of the life she had left. She was going to enjoy her friends and be a grandmother.

Upon our return from Rochester, I read as much as I could about PSP. Dr. Cutsforth-Gregory had referred us to the CurePSP.org website. I had already done some research, and the website helped fill in some of the blanks. I found references on the website for support groups in major cities of the country. I found none in Nashville, but the site also had names of people who had experienced the disease and were willing to serve as "peer supports." I called the peer support person listed for Middle Tennessee, left a detailed message, and asked her to call me. She returned my call as I was driving to Lexington, Kentucky, to meet college friends for a day of horse racing at Keeneland race track, ironically enough, the place where Kay and I became engaged.

As I drove to Lexington and listened on Bluetooth to the support person as she described her mother's struggles with PSP, I was confronted for the first time with the harsh reality of what faced us. I felt empty, weak, and distressed. I needed to talk to someone and to unburden myself somehow. When I arrived at the track, I pulled my friend Rob aside and told him what I feared lay ahead of us. I was beginning to understand. I never told Kay about that phone call because I thought it was better for her not to know.

When the drop-off in her condition occurred in the spring of 2019, I began to learn what being a caregiver really means. Kay was active and involved. She was never still. She had never been ill. Now I was watching her become nonambulatory. I was watching her fade away and become more dependent on me, and I had no way to arrest it or slow it. I was helpless.

Coach Coughlin in his *New York Times* article urges his readers to remember the caregivers. Some postings to the article from unsympathetic wags hiding behind anonymity took him to task because they said he had the financial resources to pay for help. As I was to find out, it doesn't matter how much money or help you have. If you are the primary caregiver for someone you love, someone with whom you have shared your entire adult life, caregiving is unimaginably hard.

Caregiving and love-giving exact an emotional, physical, and mental toll. They threaten your spiritual beliefs and your basic sense of self.

The tasks of caregiving are myriad and all-consuming. Kay and I had been together for a long time. She had her tasks and I had mine, and on anything of any significance, we always conferred. We never did anything against the wishes of the other. Now, almost all of those tasks and decisions had become mine alone, including decisions about her care. Many times, I felt really alone. She was there and I could run things by her, but her communication problems and a general disinterest in the minutiae of daily life made it hard to discuss things in any meaningful way. She was there, but not really there. Even with an extraordinary extended family and hordes of friends, caregiving was a solitary, lonely enterprise.

Soon after we returned to Nashville from Australia, I started helping her walk, at first just helping her a little with balance, but as time went on, she required more. For months, probably for most of the two and a half years following Easter 2019, I would walk with her. The technique we developed had me facing her and holding her left forearm with my right hand while placing my other hand either on her right forearm or waist. It was the waltz position. I would walk backward and she would walk forward. We would walk in circles around our large, octagonal living room. When her restless legs would flare up, we would walk for what seemed like hours around and around the living room, trying to bring some relief to her legs. As she declined, we had to go slower, but she could do it because of her dogged determination. She tried a walking stick, a cane with pronged legs, and the walker, but nothing proved to be a magic elixir. About the time she'd begin to master one device, her condition would worsen, and she would have to try another one. Toward the end, mostly in the last year and a half of her life, when she could not walk at all, she would just stand with Val or me holding her.

As she became less able to take care of her daily personal grooming and dressing, we settled into a daily routine. I would help her get out of bed in the morning, get her on the toilet, brush her teeth, wipe her face with a makeup removal wipe, and get her dressed. Until she drew very near to death, she picked out her own clothes every day. When she was unable to talk, she would point to a blouse, shirt, or pants in her closet. She was particular and deliberate about her dress. Even though she seldom left the house or her wheelchair, especially in the last year and a half, she was intent on looking her best for her guests, for me, and for Val. She never lost her sense of style and taste, and refused to sit around in a bathrobe, the latter a rule applied even during the isolation of the COVID pandemic.

Dressing her had its own special challenges. I discovered that the buttons on women's clothing are tiny little things, and even worse, the buttonholes are even tinier. Kay's wardrobe, both fashionable and fashionably fitted, reflected her taste. Dressing her meant struggling with skinny-legged jeans and snugly fitting pants. She had no interest in sweatpants and a baggy shirt. I admit to emitting expletives in the process of buttoning little bitty buttons in little tiny buttonholes and tugging on tight-fitting pants and sweaters.

Applying makeup was another novel challenge. Let me be clear that I do not wear makeup. It may have been suggested by some people that I would benefit from it, but I am makeup free. Further, I had never applied her makeup. In my opinion, she could have easily skipped it and relied on her natural beauty. She had never worn much makeup, but she insisted we adhere to a morning ritual that involved a dab of something called face primer, a touch of foundation, just a smidge of blush, and fashionably applied lipstick. I mastered it. I had observed her technique until she could apply it no longer, and I just did what she did. I am justifiably proud. When she emerged from the bedroom each morning, after selecting her wardrobe and directing the application of makeup, she looked like a million dollars.

On weekdays, Val would usually be there to do all or part of the morning tasks, but sometimes Kay would wake up early. If she was awake, she demanded to get out of bed. So there were many times, weekdays and all weekends, when I would be doing all the morning chores. Morning also meant making her a fruit smoothie laced with protein powder, making the bed, doing the laundry, and straightening the house. It was not hard, but doing all this and attempting to stay near enough to spring into action if she decided to ram the dining room table or a floor-to-ceiling window with the big Quantum iLevel wheelchair had its challenges. I gained a new appreciation for the daily routine of parents, especially mothers, of young children. In truth, doing the chores day after day was not the problem, but doing them while feeling sorry that Kay could not do these simple tasks herself was the bigger challenge. Thankfully, Val was with us most mornings to take the load off me. I am not whining or complaining about my duties. Plenty of people do this and much more. I am just recounting our day.

Going to bed involved somewhat the same process, but in reverse. Kay liked to go to bed late, usually around ten thirty or eleven. If she went to bed early, she was fearful she'd wake up in the middle of the night and not go back to sleep. Because of her restless legs issues, she wanted a really hot shower immediately before bedtime. Heat calmed her RLS and, without a bathtub in our house, a hot shower was the only option. As long as she could walk, we'd stand together in the shower with me holding her upright with one hand and using the other hand to bathe her with a washcloth. We would wash her hair on alternate nights. Eventually, she could no longer stand, even with me holding her. By then, we had a shower chair that her sister Susan had procured for us. The chair helped both of us in that I could then bathe her without also having to hold her up. Transfers to and from the shower and to and from the commode had their own complications, but we were always able to do them. I learned to blow-dry her hair and brush it out so that it passed inspection. I never became highly proficient at the brushing and styling, but I guess I was good enough.

There were nights when she would be so catatonic upon leaving the shower that we would have to adjust the routine. We were continuously adapting in how we handled morning and night as her condition changed and evolved. We were just making it up as we went along, but we did it. We were a good team, just as we had always been.

Even though Val was a great help in the daytime, I had no one at night or on weekends for most of the three and a half years of intensive care. I coveted the Val time. Having Val there allowed me to get the things done that had to be done, such as paying the bills, managing our finances, keeping up with Kay's complicated visitor schedule, and going to the grocery or hardware store. I gave up most of my outside activities, except my seat as chair of the Board of Trustees of the Nashville-Davidson County Public Library and my twice weekly workouts. Occasionally, I would play golf with friends, but never more than nine holes at a time and never more than a couple of times a month. I tried to have lunch with friends when I could work it in. I knew I needed to keep my body as strong as possible, and I knew I needed to stay connected with friends. I tried to cram everything that I had to do and wanted to do into that seven- or eight-hour stretch each weekday when Val was with us. I dreaded the coming of three o'clock because Val would be gone and care would all be on me again.

When I was with Kay, without the presence of Val or some other caregiver, I couldn't leave her for even the briefest time, mostly for her physical safety and the well-being of our home. But being with her was also for her psychological and emotional well-being. I think she had a lot of insecurities, both emotional and physical, even though she was good at hiding them from the outside world. She needed me or Val all the time. For those hours and days in the early days of the disease when Kay and I were alone together, we had some good times. She was sick, but she was still fun. She was engaged. She was mostly herself. I read to her a lot, we played games, and we had some laughs. I remembered anew why I loved her so much.

As her condition declined, being with her became harder. She could no longer engage in the same ways that brought joy in the early stages of the disease. We could still talk and exchange confidences. We could still kiss and hug and express our feelings. But, as was always the case, the overall trajectory of the disease was downward. I tried to think of new things to do to make her day better, to make the time pass pleasantly. As she got worse, that became harder to do. The hours dragged by, but, paradoxically, the weeks flew. It seemed that the distance between Monday morning at seven and Friday at three was a glimpse in time, but the hours comprising those weeks lasted forever. By Sunday night, after being the only caregiver for the weekend, I would fall into bed exhausted.

Pat and Bobby came for dinner often, particularly during the pandemic quarantine. Val would leave at three, and they would usually arrive around six thirty. I was fortunate to have their company, but as Kay declined, those three and a half hours between Val's leaving and their arrival came to be the hardest in the day. Those hours seemed interminable. I just wanted someone with whom I could share the burden.

In mid-February 2021, a huge snowstorm hit Nashville, making roads impassable. Neither Val nor our nighttime help could get to us, and we had four days with no help and no visitors. I think the lack of interaction with other people was hard on Kay. It was hard on me. On February 17, the fourth day of being snowbound, she was in the bedroom watching TV. She called for me as best she could, but I was in the kitchen and did not hear her. She thought she needed to pee. When I got to her, she was weeping. She felt so insecure. She needed Val or me with her constantly, not just in the same house but by her side. She didn't even like to be left alone with one of our adult children. Being locked-in verbally, physically, and somewhat emotionally must create a feeling of insecurity and vulnerability that most of us cannot imagine.

A few nights later, she wanted me to hold her while we watched TV. She was sitting in her wheelchair. In the past, I had held her on my lap on occasion, but by early 2021, even that had become problematic. As she sat in her chair, I tried to hold her. It was awkwardly and clumsily done, but as events unfolded over the ensuing months, holding her as she sat in her wheelchair became more frequent.

Incontinence and irregularity were always a problem. I felt so sorry for her. A friend who had lost his wife to cancer told me soon after Kay was diagnosed about all the things that he had done for his wife, including cleaning her up after a bowel movement. I recoiled. Oooh! I didn't think I could do that. But I could, I did, and I did not mind it. She needed me, and I was there.

Sometimes, she would get angry at me. As the disease took away more and more of her physical vitality, she became more emotionally fragile. Something that would have been of little significance to her in normal times, or even earlier in the disease, might become intensely disturbing to her. She wanted to be able to depend on me constantly. She could get mad at me when she couldn't get mad at anyone else. She couldn't be angry at her friends who were spending so much time trying to give her enjoyment. She couldn't be angry at Pat, who was coming to cook our dinner night after night. She couldn't be angry at our children or our grandchildren. It was not in her nature to direct anger at the medical professionals trying to help her. She had nowhere to direct her frustration, so I became the recipient of most of it. I was her safe place.

On December 1, 2019, I wrote in my journal that she was mad at me. The same thing had happened the preceding Friday, which was the day after Thanksgiving, and then again on Saturday. First, she got mad because I was taking too long to clean up after Thanksgiving dinner. Then, she was mad because I was texting with one of her friends, who was simply inquiring about Kay's condition. The previous weekend, she got mad at me because I hadn't purchased a motorized wheelchair. In mid-October, she'd been fitted for the Quantum iLevel wheelchair, but we had to wait for it to be delivered. She was not in a mood to wait, and I was the one whom she believed had been derelict in getting the chair. I immediately went online and bought a smaller motorized chair so she could have conveyance until the big chair arrived. There were plenty of other times when anger boiled over.

I really had a hard time with my emotions when she showed anger toward me. I could rationalize why she was mad and why she was mad at me, but emotionally I had a hard time absorbing it. As I went through my journal entries since her death, I was struck by how many describe some episode of anger at me. The mad spells were infrequent compared to the stretches of time when she was dealing with the disease with her usual composure, but I think absorbing the anger was just so emotionally difficult for me that I must have recorded those instances disproportionately to other events. I couldn't get mad at her or argue with her or walk away. She needed me and I had to be there for her. I didn't always write down the good times, but I couldn't help but write down the hard times. Maybe recording them was my own way of unleashing my emotions without damage to her or others.

By the end of 2019, I was starting to break down. She was becoming increasingly difficult to care for. I was sleep deprived and exhausted. I had no help at night or on weekends. On December 3, 2019, I wrote in my journal, *We don't live, we just survive; we just exist.* It would be another two years of just existing before the disease took her. We were just getting started.

I went through a range of emotions that I have learned are normal, to the extent anything about this experience is normal, and should be expected. I don't know which emotions came first and which came later. They came and went. Nothing was linear. I was angry. I was tired. I was sad. I was sorry. I was frustrated I couldn't do more. When I was in Rosemary Beach in September 2020, I wrote in my journal, *Caregiving is exhausting—holding her up, transferring her, walking with her, trying to keep her from becoming frustrated, trying to communicate, trying to think of things to do to make the time pass.*

As time passed, I started asking the existential questions. What role does God play in this? I grew up in a traditional rural Southern Baptist church. Kay grew up in an urban Catholic church and went to Catholic school through ninth grade. After we married, we strayed from the orthodoxies of our youth to more questioning, probing spiritualities.

Neither of us was sure of an all-knowing omnipotent God in control of us and the universe. We both embraced the idea of a greater power, but had little understanding of what that means. We both saw God, whoever and whatever God is, as a loving, caring God, but not necessarily a God exercising control over our lives.

Even though I didn't initially blame God for Kay's illness, as time went on, I started asking questions of God. I got mad at God. I yelled at him. I asked him, "What is your plan?" I asked, "Do you even have a plan? Do you have a clue what is going on here?" I asked him, "If you are so all-mighty, all-powerful, and loving, why are you inflicting this suffering upon this person, who has never harmed anyone and always tried to help people and be what I thought you wanted all of us to be?" I had to have someone to rage at, and I figured God should be first in line. After Kay's death, someone gave me *A Grief Observed* by C.S. Lewis. I had read Lewis years ago, but not at all in many years. As I read his lament over losing his wife, Joy, I was struck by the following:

> "Meanwhile, where is God? This is one of the most disquieting symptoms. When you are happy, so happy that you have no sense of needing Him, so happy that you are tempted to feel His claims upon you as an interruption, if you remember yourself and turn to Him with gratitude and praise, you will be—or so it feels—welcomed with open arms. But go to Him when your need is desperate, when all other help is vain, and what do you find? A door slammed in your face, and a sound of bolting and double bolting on the inside. After that, silence."

One of my good friends, Joe, is an ordained clergy who has spent his entire career in prison ministry, primarily death row ministry. He has puzzled over these questions and the injustices of our existence as much as anyone. When Kay's condition worsened, Joe and I started having lunch together once a week or, in place of lunch during the COVID quarantine, taking long walks down a rural lane close to his house. We talked about my disappointment in God and my anger at his seeming disinterest in Kay's condition.

I have another close friend, Don, who has a PhD in ethics from Vanderbilt Divinity School. I asked all these questions of Don. I never found the answers because there are no answers. Don said God is love, and that's all we need to know. Joe said there is a God. He has seen evidence of God in action. Both indulged me. They let me ask the questions. They let me vent without judging me or subjecting me to a pedantic that would have been counterproductive.

Joe directed me to a Bible study group at our church that was just beginning to delve into the Book of Job. I discovered in the Bible study class that Job had cursed God too. Job asked all these questions. In the end, Job became reconciled with God. C.S. Lewis followed the same path and found the same reconciliation. I suppose I did too. I came to accept anew, as I had always believed, that God is not a puppeteer. We live in a random universe in which unfortunate things, bad things, unfair things, happen. God is not there to keep the wolf from the door. He is love, and sometimes we just need to know that we are loved. Maybe God was speaking to me through these two friends and Job. Maybe he wasn't. I don't know. But to have these two good friends to whom I could vent my frustration with or disbelief in God without being judged was an enormous help.

There were multiple times when I was certain that I could not go on. It was February of 2021 before we found dependable nighttime help. Friends and family were with us for dinner many nights, but only Val and I could do the physical work of taking care of Kay. Further, Kay didn't want anyone but Val and me taking care of her. When Lauren was still in Australia, I once called all three of our adult children together via FaceTime and poured myself out to them, and then asked what more they could do to help. They were doing all they could do, but it wasn't enough. The burden rested on me. I was getting tired. Mostly, I just needed to unpack it all with them. I just had to unload.

In the spring of 2020, it had been a year since Kay started needing round-the-clock care. The COVID-19 virus had hit, restricting everyone's social interaction, including ours. She was getting worse, and I felt powerless to do anything about it. One day, I decided that I wouldn't let the disease get the best of me. I started thinking of all the wonderful things in this world. I started thinking of all the blessings in my life and in Kay's life and in our life together. I decided to write down those blessings. Every night for a couple of months, after getting Kay in bed for the night, I would sit down for five minutes and write down one thing from that day for which I was thankful. On March 9, I wrote that I was thankful for a good night's sleep the previous night. On Wednesday, March 18, I wrote that I was thankful for green grass. Other entries included a warm day, the pear tree in our front yard starting to bloom, John Prine, old friends, my mother, a text message from a friend, and a walk in the neighborhood. One night, I wrote that Kay said to me, "You are a great caregiver." I was thankful for that. Another day, April 4, I wrote that Kay had walked down the steps to the treadmill and said triumphantly, "I did it!" Another day, I wrote that I was thankful for Kay. They were simple things. They were things for which I was truly thankful, and writing them down made me feel better.

In the early days after diagnosis, Lauren suggested that Kay and I see a therapist friend of hers named Laurel. Kay and I consented. We went together twice. Then Laurel asked each of us to come separately. We did that, but Kay didn't like it. She did not want to talk about the disease. She did not want to talk about death. She did not want to talk about her feelings. She never went back. I didn't go back either for a while, mainly because Kay did not want me to go back. But, as she became worse, I would get so tired and emotionally drained that I decided that talking to Laurel in a safe, nonjudgmental, confidential space might be good.

Laurel was not the first person from whom I had sought professional help. After I started looking for nighttime and weekend help, mid-January 2020, eighteen months after diagnosis, someone suggested that I consult with a social worker named Kelly at Vanderbilt Medical

Center. Kelly works almost exclusively with Parkinson's patients and their families. I contacted her. We met once and talked on the phone once. I thought she was really good, very comforting, exactly what I needed just then. At the time, my main goal in talking to her was to understand what lay ahead of us and how to find dependable care to supplement Val. Kelly suggested that I attend a group session of family members of atypical parkinsonism patients. I went. No one in the session was dealing with PSP. Some had it easier than I did, but some were living in worlds far worse than mine. For some, their loved ones were not as sick as Kay, while others had unbelievable situations with which they were dealing. I am not much on group dynamics of that sort and never went back. My sympathies were with these people. I don't think any of them had sufficient resources at their disposal to handle their situations. I came away feeling that even though Kay was cursed, we were blessed in many ways. Dealing with these diseases without any help or emotional support seemed to me to be a bridge too far.

The first time I went back to Laurel, I didn't tell Kay until I came home after the appointment. By then, we were well into mid-2020. She was already spending most of her time in the Quantum iLevel wheelchair. When I told her about my session with Laurel, she was livid. She felt that I should have asked her permission. She felt betrayed. I think she thought I was sharing emotions and secrets with the therapist that I should not be sharing with anyone other than her. I was. But, I couldn't share all my emotions about the disease and my emotional exhaustion with Kay.

It seemed that Kay did not want a therapist knowing about her life, our life together and the hardships of the moment. I don't know what she really thought because of her difficulty in expressing herself, but I am glad I went to the therapist. I don't think Laurel employed any great therapy techniques with me, but she helped. She just listened. She allowed me to be angry, guilty, and remorseful. I felt that I was a terrible caregiver. I felt that I had not been what I should have been as a husband over all our years. I had regrets. I had sadness. She let me talk and helped me not only understand my feelings but also come to know that it was okay to have them.

Laurel offered two tangible suggestions that I put into practice. She suggested that I see my primary care physician and ask for a mild anti-depressant. I resisted. She didn't press me on it, but she persuasively observed that depression can surface in different ways. I was not clini-cally depressed. Nobody was thinking or saying that, but there was no doubt that Kay and I were living through an emotionally draining time. She urged me to give it a try. She said the dosage would be very light, and it might just take the edge off a little. Eventually, I did try it. I don't know how much it helped, but it didn't hurt. I am glad I did it.

Laurel's other suggestion, which I took to heart, was that Kay and I collaborate on the life story we had related in part to her in our joint visit. I guess it is standard practice for therapists to begin by learning the life story of each patient. Laurel asked, among other things, how we met, how we made our way to Nashville, and how our careers evolved. She was fascinated by our life story. At least, she feigned fascination. Isn't that what therapists are supposed to do? She said to me in our later solo sessions that Kay and I should write it all down. She wanted us to preserve our life story. Just sit down and do it. I had never thought of our story as being anything unique, but I took her advice. I never told Kay where the idea originated, but I suggested we do it. She seized upon the idea, and we did it.

My father and most of my family and friends in the small town near where I grew up spent their last days in a nursing home. It seemed to be the way of things in LaCenter, Kentucky. I guess the folks who lived there were lucky to have such a facility. Every time I walked into that place to see Daddy or others, I could feel the sickness and sadness engulf me. Every time I walked out, I would feel a weight lifted from my shoulders and a cloud blow away. I hated the smell and the hopelessness. It was a depressing place. Thankfully, Kay never had to go to any sort of institutional living situation. She didn't even go to a hospital. We made it all the way through her illness without having to be separated by an institutional living arrangement. Something else for which to be thankful.

But, even though a nursing home or other institutional living facility was never part of our life together, I sometimes felt as if our house was a mini-nursing home. Kay's unrelenting spirit and the frequency of visits from friends and family made every day brighter, but I nevertheless felt a lingering, overarching sadness not even our home and all our blessings could totally wipe away. I always thought people who came to see us must have whistled a sigh of relief as they drove away from our house, just as I did years ago when I left the nursing home.

I kept asking myself why I was always so tired. Val was with us seven to eight hours a day. She was dependable and trustworthy. I didn't worry about Kay when Val was there. Her presence should have provided me the respite that I needed, but I never felt truly rested. No matter what I did to get away, my spirit and mind remained with Kay and the ever-present disease. Sadly, Kay could never leave it even when a friend or relative got her away from home for a few hours. The disease was always there. The clouds sometimes allowed a few rays of sunshine through, but they never cleared. All of this weighed on me.

I went through a phase of anger. I had no one to be angry at or with. As I said earlier, the only one to whom I could direct anger was God, and that didn't seem to be getting me anywhere. I couldn't be angry with Kay. For the most part, I rarely showed anger toward her. So I just bottled it up. I would bottle it up and let it out when the bottle couldn't hold anymore. Sometimes, I would get angry or sad or frustrated—who knows which of these—or other emotions, and say terrible things about family members, friends, caregivers, doctors, hospice workers, and plenty of others, particularly a few of Kay's friends who claimed to be close friends who were not darkening her door. Sometimes it would just come out. I didn't express my emotions face-to-face to the subject of my disgust. I was more prone to gripe behind their backs, a cowardly way to express anger, but since it was unjustified, I am grateful I did it that way. I regret all that.

The worst-of-the-worst fits of anger involved Pat and Bobby. One Sunday afternoon in the spring of 2020, Pat suggested that I go watch our grandsons play golf. At the time, they were nine and eleven years old and, like most boys their age, playing every sport invented. On this day, they were participating in a golf tournament. Kay and I both enjoyed supporting them and watching them play sports, but in the spring of 2020, her condition would to have allowed her to go to a golf course and follow the boys around. Because I had skipped almost all their sporting events that spring to stay with Kay, I thought going to watch the boys play that day would be all right. Pat said she would stay with Kay. It would be only a few hours on a Sunday afternoon, and I thought Kay would be okay. So I went.

Kay was irritated with me when I left and did not want me to go. When I returned home after being gone no more than a couple of hours, she was mad at me. I cannot say from where the anger came—perhaps because she couldn't go, perhaps because I had left her, perhaps because I had a moment of joy that she couldn't have, perhaps because I could go and be a grandpa and she couldn't go and be a MomMom. Wherever it came from, in hindsight I guess I don't blame her. At the time, though, her anger was more than I could abide. I exploded, but not at her. I couldn't do that. I had to direct it somewhere else. So, when we sat down to eat that evening, something set me off, and I slammed a wine bottle on the table, spilling wine all over the table, Pat, Bobby, and me, and I screamed at poor, innocent Bobby. Thankfully, he understood the outburst, as did Pat. What went through my mind was that I was spending day after day, hour after hour taking care of her, and she was begrudging me two hours to watch our grandsons play golf. I deemed it unfair and ungrateful. It was a tense moment. It was another moment I regret. In the kindest, most understanding way possible, Pat said, "Why don't you take a break?" I went outside and sat alone for fifteen or twenty minutes, getting my emotions under control, and then came back, apologized, and had dinner.

My mind sometimes played strange games with me. Sometime in early 2021, some nine or ten months before Kay died, I pulled out a Bible for my Bible Buddies Class, the one that had introduced me to Job's anguish. The Bible was one I had in high school and college days. Out of the Bible fell a picture of a girlfriend of my youth, named Becky. She was a summer fling after my sophomore year in college, long before I met Kay. I had no hint the picture was there. Looking at it gave me an overwhelming feeling of nostalgia, and I couldn't stop thinking about her for several days. I hadn't seen or heard from her in over fifty years, nor do I have any idea where she is or how to contact her. I doubt she looks as pretty now as she did then at age eighteen. I barely knew her then, as it had been a two-week summer thing. She evaporated from my life long ago, but seeing her picture evoked that same adolescent gooey feeling in my stomach that I'd had when we were together.

The Becky sighting brought to mind my high school sweetheart, Sally. Once again, I experienced that same feeling in the pit of my stomach, just like with Becky. Becky was a fleeting moment, but Sally and I had gone together throughout our junior and senior years in high school. Our closeness was special, but other than a brief conversation at our fiftieth high school reunion that Kay and I attended in July of 2016, I had had no contact with her since my first year in college.

For several weeks, these thoughts of young love overwhelmed me. It was as if I had rediscovered my youth and the infatuation that comes with it. Then, I became homesick for the little country place where I grew up. I hadn't been back home since my father died in 2006.

I discussed all these thoughts and feelings with Laurel. She said to lean into them. She said don't bury them. Luxuriate in them, without guilt. They will go away. I did, and they did.

Now, thinking back to those early days of 2021, maybe my subconscious was offering me a respite from my grief and weariness. I just wanted to be happy. When the picture fell out of that Bible, happiness fell out with it. There is no better happiness than first love and those teenage years. There is no sweeter love than love of home, the place of origins. I was in love with memories, with feelings. I guess my psyche was saying I needed those feelings. I was tired and missing Kay. My mind was calling for something to fill the void. It was screaming for escape. Maybe it was preparing me for the feeling of nostalgia and longing that I feel now for Kay and our life together, now that she is gone and that life is gone.

I was confident during the period of caregiving that I had all my faculties about me and that I was "on my game." Looking back now, I am not so sure. I did a decent enough job scheduling all the people who wanted to visit Kay, keeping her prescriptions filled and the medications organized, taking care of all the financial affairs of the house and family, and generally running a household. As I look back on it, most of the time I was in a fog. I had to be careful about making notes and keeping careful financial records because I couldn't remember what I'd done five minutes after doing it. A few times we were overdrawn in one of our bank accounts. Occasionally, I would forget to pay a bill. You may say that this happens to all of us as we age. That may be true, but this was much worse. I couldn't remember where I put things or where I was supposed to be. I was not demented, but continuously preoccupied. Even when I would get away to do something with a friend or friends, I was never truly "away." Kay and her struggles were always on my mind.

I've worked hard all my life. I've often been physically and mentally tired. But I never knew what it was like to be physically, mentally, and emotionally exhausted. Each night during those years of her illness, I would literally fall into bed. Each morning, I would wake up knowing that the day ahead was going to be just as trying as the day before. I would be so very tired, but I tried to hide it from Kay and others. I wanted to be, and had to be, really strong for her. She did not take a charitable view of weakness, complaining or sloughing of duty, and my travails were nothing compared to hers. I tried to take it one day at a time, just as she was doing, and to notice all the blessings of our lives as the days piled one on top of the other.

Part of what made caregiving so hard was the indefiniteness of it. How long could this go on? What was Kay's condition going to be as the disease progressed? I had no timetable to guide me. I interrogated more than one person who had been down this road, but never got answers that were helpful to me. The best came from Ann Patchett, whose father had died of PSP. She was not his primary caregiver, but she was with him a great deal during his decline. She told me of his condition toward the end of his life and chronicled his decline for me. I needed to know and knowing helped. Of course, the disease affects everyone differently, and life spans with the disease vary so the experience of others might not have been any help. Even so, I kept searching for guidance.

In looking at CurePSP.org, I had found that life spans with the disease can be as long as ten years, but that the average is closer to six. Dr. Cutsforth-Gregory had said ten years. Kay first showed signs of the disease in 2016, maybe as early as 2015. She died in 2021. That is a lifespan of somewhere between five and six years, and three and a half years from diagnosis. If we had known in June of 2018 when we were at Mayo Clinic that a mere three and a half years later she would be an emaciated skeleton of herself, we would have been even more devastated than we were that day. Maybe, it was better that we didn't know.

I had times when I wanted it to end. I feel guilty admitting those feelings, but not knowing if we were facing years, months, or weeks was sometimes unbearable. When seeking guidance and predictability from doctors and other PSP caregivers, I would always couch my inquiries of "how much longer" in terms of preparing for the next stage. But truthfully, some of wanting to know was wanting someone to tell me how much longer this would last. In hindsight, I don't know whether a more definite timetable would have helped. Knowing how the end looked certainly would have depressed me more than I already was. Maybe, "one day at a time" was the answer. I don't know the answer.

Throughout this whole experience, particularly now that she is gone, I have often been praised for my dedication to her and my diligence as a caregiver. I say thank you. I do appreciate people saying nice things like that, but inside I am saying hogwash. I did what I had to do. I did what anyone would do with the capacity to do it. I think of my parents often. Mother has been dead thirty-eight years and Daddy has been dead fifteen years. I think about how hard they worked. I think about the load they carried without the conveniences of today. They did what they had to do, and they did it for years. Mother took care of her mother, my grandmother, after she had a debilitating stroke. She did what she had to do. That's all that I did. Institutionalizing Kay was never even considered. She did not need it. Short of institutionalization, there was no alternative but to take care of her the best I could. Then, I consider Kay and all that she endured. She is the hero. She is the one who showed what the human spirit is capable of overcoming. All the credit goes to her.

13

Caregivers

Get help

One of the immediate responses to the emails that Kay and I sent upon her diagnosis was a peppering of advice to me: *Get help.* It was well-meaning advice and carried the unmistakable ring of truth, but as I was to learn, naively given. Finding and keeping good help is not as easy as acknowledging that you need it. I was to find that securing reliable, competent help was a winding, bumpy road that did not find its terminus until four months before her death. But help comes in different flavors, and this chapter and the two that follow deal with the reality of help—paid caregivers, hospice, and friends. Those chapters, particularly this one and the one to follow, are my attempt at a primer on help, potentially of value to anyone staring any chronic debilitating disease in the face.

The search for help was complicated by Kay not wanting help. She didn't want a strange person in our home performing intimate, personal tasks. She wanted me to be the help. Fortunately, in the spring of 2019 while Kay could still walk, talk and feed herself, we found Val. In a sense, Val and Kay grew together within the disease. Val was a perfect fit with Kay. She is smart, fun, engaging, attractive, and quick with a laugh, all the traits Kay loved in her friends. Val promptly learned the ways of our household. She could figure out how to do almost anything, never creating a burden for us. She seemed to instinctively know what needed to be done and when and how to do it.

What about this special person Val? As previously noted, Kay began having more pronounced balance difficulties in the spring of 2019, around Easter of that year. Val was relatively young at thirty-seven, but a veteran caregiver of some twenty years. She had been sitting on weekdays with an elderly lady in the community and with Bobby's brother Joel on Sundays. As a result, Pat saw Val regularly. When the elderly lady died in the spring of 2019, Pat immediately alerted us to Val's availability.

We responded to Pat that we didn't need anyone. Kay was resistant and I thought I could take care of her. Maybe I didn't want to confront reality. Like Kay, maybe I didn't want another person in the house. We were doing pretty well and cherishing our moments together. I was one step behind the need.

Sometimes, you need the perspective of someone not in the eye of the storm. Pat could see more clearly what was coming and the toll that it was already taking. My reluctance along with Kay's resistance are lessons for any caregiver. Heed the advice of friends and family, and do not continue with caregiving until you can no longer physically and emotionally do it. Pain doctors will tell pain patients to get ahead of the pain with appropriate pain medication rather than waiting until the pain is unbearable. It's the same with caregiving. Stay ahead of the need if you have the resources and wherewithal to do it.

At Pat's insistence, we agreed to meet with Val. She came to the house and talked with us. We liked her so much that we hired her on the spot. Kay took to Val immediately, and they soon became fast friends. When Val would arrive in the morning, I could disappear for a while and refuel. I knew that when Val was with Kay, she would be cared for with love. Val would usually arrive in time for the morning ritual that I have already described. Once all that was done, the chatter began. Then came laughter. Then more chatter. Kay and Val shared their secrets, with neither ever divulging what was said. Even now, in Kay's absence, Val is not telling. Kay gave Val advice about all manner of things, including what to do with the rest of her life and how to handle her boyfriend. I am pretty sure some of her advice seemed outrageous to Val and some of it was probably wise and insightful in ways Val had never considered.

Kay never gave up the idea of being active even though her body eventually refused to follow her lead, so Val became her surrogate and proxy. Kay liked to shop. She liked to garden. She liked to cook. She liked art and beauty. She liked anything that involved action and movement. Kay would shop online and shop in stores with Val as her accomplice and facilitator. They would go to the botanical gardens, the art museum, and the music museum.

Kay would think up little tasks she wanted Val to do around the house, such as touching up all the baseboards in the house that had been rammed with Kay's wheelchair. She told Val to do it in secret without telling me. She was a little embarrassed about ramming walls and baseboards and thought if she and Val touched them up surreptitiously, I would never notice. She had Val pot plants and flowers, identify birds in our backyard, and make fruit pies and cheesecake. One day in advance of some holiday, Kay taught her to make a fruit trifle. Not only had Val never made a fruit trifle, she'd never heard of it. They made it and it was beautiful. But the amazing thing was that Kay was teaching Val how to do a lot of this after she'd lost her ability to talk. In other words, she directed Val to make a fruit trifle without saying a word. Never underestimate Kay. She taught Val her tricks. She enlisted Val to help make the legacy books that she gave the family. In the early days of the disease, Kay could always think of something to do, and Val would willingly do whatever Kay wanted with the same joy that Kay found in conceiving the idea. They were partners in crime from the day Val arrived until Kay left us.

Kay had spent her whole life connecting people, being a mentor to people, and making lives better through her friendships. Even in her decline toward death, she continued to connect and mentor, focusing mostly on Val. I believe, and Val would say, that Kay changed her life. Kay opened worlds to her that she didn't know existed. She connected Val to her network of interesting, fun, and exciting women, establishing relationships among these women and Val that hopefully will be a part of her life forever. They had a sweet and heartwarming relationship. I know Kay was much happier in her final days because of Val's companionship. If those two had met ten years earlier when Kay was in her prime, they would have shaken the world.

By fall of 2019, I could see that Kay was getting worse. Val was invaluable, but I was coming to the realization that we were going to need more. We were fortunate to have long-term care insurance, and in the fall of 2019, I decided it was time to use it. It turned out to be a blessing, but not without a lot of work and frustration along the way.

Long-term care policies seem to be written in a variety of ways. Kay's policy covered not only institutional care but also in-home care. The policy required that any in-home caregiver qualifying us for reimbursement must be affiliated with a qualifying, licensed caregiving agency. Since Val had no such affiliation, the insurance benefits were unavailable to reimburse us for Val. We were fortunate to have the resources to pay her, but I wanted any additional help we might need to be covered by the insurance.

In the fall of 2019, I had a lot to learn about in-home caregiving. First, I had to learn the vocabulary. As with anything in the modern American health care system, nothing is straightforward. Nothing is simple. I began my search by getting the names of some home health agencies and calling them. Seems simple enough, right? It turns out that these folks do not actually do daily hands-on, in-home health care, despite the name. They send people to your home to render medical services like physical therapy, dialysis, and administration of medication. They will come and do baths, but only once or twice a week. They don't provide daily care. Why don't they provide actual in-home daily care? They don't because Medicare and Medicaid will not pay for it. These agencies are looking for the deepest pockets. That's the way our health care system works. No money, no care. Welcome to the burgeoning Nashville health care industry, the home of for-profit health care, where health-care millionaires and billionaires are minted every day while people who do not have the resources struggle to take care of loved ones. Please pardon the rant. Without the resources we had, I could not have survived. What of others who must deal with PSP or a host of other such diseases without adequate resources to pay for care? We needed daily care, not weekly therapy. I was shopping in the wrong aisle.

I next found myself in another fraternity of players. I needed to be looking for "home care" agencies, not "home health" agencies. I assumed our choices in this world would be severely limited due to lack of government subsidy. Not so. I soon found that there are over four hundred such agencies in the Middle Tennessee area alone. Through our daughter Jennifer, who is associate general counsel at the Vanderbilt Medical Center, we made our way to Vanderbilt Home Care Services. Vanderbilt qualified under Kay's long-term care policy.

Having found an agency that would meet our needs, I now needed to dig deeper into the insurance policy. All my dealings with the insurance company were satisfactory, but I had to learn to play by their rules, including protocols as simple as the proper way to contact our claims representative. Once I got the protocol down, it wasn't difficult, albeit occasionally time-consuming. First, we had to establish that she could not perform at least two of the Activities of Daily Living, a defined term, meaning bathing, dressing, toileting, transferring, continence and eating. The policy also required that we satisfy a 180-day Elimination Period before benefits could be paid, that is, 180 days of unreimbursed care from a qualifying agency. Under Kay's policy, service for one hour for one day a week counted as seven days for purposes of satisfying the 180-day requirement.

Now that we had an agency and understood the rules, we started having Vanderbilt send someone each Monday so we could satisfy the Elimination Period. Val came the other four days each week. Kay and I still had our weekends, afternoons and evenings together. Vanderbilt was very accommodating in this regard. Providing care on a one-day-a-week basis is probably not their sweet spot. By the spring of 2020, we were on the verge of satisfying the Elimination Period when the COVID-19 virus hit. I discontinued the Vanderbilt service rather than take the chance that one of Vanderbilt's people would transmit the COVID-19 virus to Kay or me. Val continued to come, and we increased her hours to five days a week. Of course, she could have infected us as well, but by the spring of 2020, we needed her. Certainly, for Val, the need for a dependable paycheck motivated her willingness to continue coming, but I think the overriding factor was that she and Kay had formed such a bond that Val was unwilling to leave Kay.

By summer of 2020, I found myself in need of more help. I was taking care of all the afternoon, nighttime, and weekend caregiving. It had been almost two years since diagnosis and eighteen months since the intensity of providing care had ramped up. By summer, I was feeling a little better about the risk of contracting the COVID-19 virus. Masking seemed to be working, and I needed some help regardless of the risk. We were only a week or two away from satisfying the Elimination Period, but we were confronting a deadline when the Elimination Period requirement would be reinstated and we would have to start all over again. It was time.

We never really loved any of the caregivers that Vanderbilt sent on a once-a-week basis, although in hindsight after experiences with other agencies, they were not so bad. I started asking friends and acquaintances about other care agencies. Eventually, I settled on three agencies to interview. I chose the smallest one, thinking we would get more personalized service from them.

I had this rosy notion that the care agencies had a stable of people just waiting to be assigned duty, just waiting to fill our every need. I also had the idea that we could meet with potential caregivers before they were actually assigned to us by the agency and select the proper fit, just as we had engaged Val. Boy, was I wrong! Here's how it really works. The agency typically sends an intake person to talk to you, either by phone or in person. The intake person asks you a bunch of relevant questions. I always liked the intake person. Kay didn't like any of them. The intake person would gain your trust and begin a relationship, and then you would never see that person again. Then, after you contract with the agency, you get a phone call telling you someone you've never met will be at your house that day— no introduction, no interview, and no selection—just a warm body showing up on your doorstep. In our case, sometimes that person would know something about the disease and Kay, but usually that person would show up with no knowledge at all. I would find myself explaining the whole situation while wondering why the intake person had gathered all the information in the first place.

Not surprisingly, Kay didn't like any of the people who were sent by the agencies, and I didn't like most of them. Her world was fragile and insecure, and then one day, a perfect stranger would show up at her front door to spend extended hours with her in her own home performing the most personal of tasks for her. Kay would sometimes get confused about events of the day, not do well processing current information, and not even realize that the appearance of a caregiver was imminent. She was depending on me and consistency, so when a strange person would just show up, she didn't like it. We were probably too picky with the caregivers who were sent to us. I think if we had been part of a process, we would have had an easier time, and the caregiver would have had an easier time as well.

The agencies, by and large, didn't have consistent workforces. They seemed to operate more like employment agencies. When we had someone quit or be absent, the agency would look for someone new. Most of the people we had were people who had never worked for that agency in the past. I am overgeneralizing for sure, but we probably had fifteen to twenty different people, and my characterization would apply to most of them. Counting Vanderbilt, we used three different agencies, and I talked to one other agency that seemed to me to be reputable. We didn't use the fourth agency because the intake person was honest enough to tell me that the agency lacked the personnel to serve us properly. Vanderbilt was better than most and really helpful as Kay's condition grew worse. I thought the others were exploitative of their people and sketchy in their operations.

Finally, at the end of January 2021, one of the agencies, not Vanderbilt, sent us someone who was quite good. She was coming five evenings a week, which took a tremendous load off me. After several weeks of acclimation, Kay came to accept her. Things were better. The COVID-19 virus was still around by then, but in January and February of 2021, Kay and I received our vaccinations. I was aware that our new evening caregiver had not been vaccinated, but I was so relieved to have someone that I didn't press it. Then, a new variant of the virus showed up, and I became more apprehensive. Finally, on July 25, 2021, I couldn't stand it any longer and confronted her about being unvaccinated and asked that she get the shots. I thought this was a reasonable request, given the nature of her work, but by July of 2021, my abilities to self-regulate my emotions and parse my words were pretty well shot. My request must have sounded like an order to her and she flatly refused, leading to a heated exchange between us glaring at each other across the dining room table. As I faced off with her that night, I knew I was stabbing myself in the gut. Even as I was debating with her, I was saying to myself, "Why are you doing this?" I had a sick feeling in the pit of my stomach because I didn't think I could go back to full-time afternoon and nighttime duty. I just couldn't do it. She quit the next day. I talked to the agency and begged them not to let her quit. That is how desperate I was. It didn't work. The agency found someone new who started three weeks later, came for three days, and quit. That three-week hiatus was really hard. At that point, Kay only had four months to live and taking care of her was difficult and heartbreaking. I never heard from that agency again.

By now, I had proven to myself that my searches at other agencies were ineffective and called Vanderbilt. They were understanding and helpful, and the next day sent Keshia, who was with us the last four months of Kay's life. Keshia had been with Vanderbilt for years. She knew her craft, took care of Kay, and endeared herself to Kay and the family. She was a consistent presence until Kay died. Vanderbilt also sent Jovan on the weekends. She was good and dependable, and also came until the end. Those two women were like a cold drink of water after a long, hot summer day. I will forever be grateful.

One more point needs to be made about the caregiver world. Even though we had a hard time finding someone that we liked from the choices we were given, I have tremendous respect for the people who do this work. They labor under difficult circumstances for low pay. The people coming in the evening were probably working all day at a day-time job. Many appeared to be living on the very edge of poverty. We might come to like someone, and the next night that person, with very little notice, wouldn't be there because her car malfunctioned and she had no money to fix it until payday, or she needed to care for someone in her own family and had no one but herself to do it. The work can be physically demanding. The stress can be draining. They are in someone else's home where they may not be wanted by one member of the family, tolerated by another, and welcomed by another. The family members themselves may not get along with each other. They may be unreasonable in their demands of the caregiver. The home may be unkempt and substandard. They are asked to deliver loving care to someone who quite likely is going to die. They have to have some emotional barrier that allows them to give care with empathy and kindness, but not feel the loss when it inevitably comes.

It was hard for Val when Kay died. They had become best friends. I hope to always stay in touch with her. She is a member of our family now. We also loved Keshia and Jovan, and I think they loved Kay. One day not long after Kay died, I looked out my front door to see a car that I didn't recognize pulling into the driveway. It was Keshia. She got out of the car, came to me, and gave me a big hug. She said that she just wanted to come and give me that hug. She was grieving too. I think she needed that hug just as much as I did.

14

Hospice

It was a very good way to die

Hospice deserves its own chapter. We began hospice care on January 6, 2021, ten months before Kay's death. Several people told us we should start using hospice. I had been in no hurry. I thought it would have negative symbolism for Kay. Toward the end of 2020, I raised the issue with her, explaining that hospice was just another way to get medical care. She agreed.

Acting upon advice of our daughter Jennifer, I picked Alive Hospice as our provider. I interviewed three other providers, but they were all for-profit agencies. Alive is a nonprofit agency. We were advised by friends and acquaintances that we would probably be more satisfied with the care if we picked the nonprofit agency over the others.

My naive and uneducated vision of hospice was a nurse at Kay's bedside constantly. That is not how it works. Hospice facilitates do-it-yourself dying. The greatest advantage to hospice, in my opinion, is that the hospice professionals are there when you really need them and not there when you don't. Even though I didn't trust that Val, Keshia, Jovan, and I were capable of caring for Kay through the final days, I found that we were capable. Hospice didn't need to be at Kay's bedside constantly as long as we were there and the hospice professionals were available. The way to get 24/7 attention is to go to a hospital or a nursing home. I wanted no part of either. The alternative is to do it yourself with professional, knowledgeable support. That is what hospice does for you.

Medicare is the pivot point that drives the way in which hospice works. Kay had a Medicare Advantage plan that covered all her medical expenses, except co-pays and deductibles. Under hospice, Medicare switches entirely to funding of the hospice care. Medicare no longer funds your primary care physician or your specialists of choice. I didn't understand that until it was explained during the intake process. Accepting hospice care meant that Medicare would no longer pay for us to see the doctors we knew and trusted. It meant we had to put our faith in another care team with whom we had no experience and in whom we had not built any trust.

We were already dealing with a terminal illness. My nerves were frayed. Kay was fraught with insecurities. Introducing a new uncertainty into our lives was almost more than we could handle. Her primary care physician had been with us from the beginning, and we loved her. We had recently switched to a new neurologist and loved her too. And, most importantly, we needed her RLS doctor. The other two doctors could not really help Kay, but her restless legs episodes needed continual attention. It seemed like a huge leap of faith.

Just as I had to learn the mechanics of the home care business, I now had to learn the mechanics of hospice. Kay was eligible for hospice because her condition was untreatable and incurable and would lead to her death in the foreseeable future. I think the technical rule is that death is expected within six months. Of course, no one knew when Kay would die, but we knew it was inevitable. If she had lived longer than the ten months that she was in hospice care, she could have stayed with hospice as long the hospice doctor and nurse could certify she had not recovered and death remained imminent.

We were assigned a hospice team composed of a palliative care doctor, whom we only saw one time; a registered nurse; a social worker;

and a chaplain. They became responsible for Kay's care, but they also stayed in contact with her other doctors whom she was no longer seeing. The nurse and the social worker came to our house as often as needed. At first, they came fortnightly. As Kay's condition worsened, they came once a week and then twice a week. There was also a nurse on call at all times. The on-call nurse was not Kay's nurse and, in fact, we saw three different on-call nurses and never saw the same person twice. But a knowledgeable, competent nurse was always there within a half hour of our call the few times we needed someone at night or on weekends.

In my reasoning knowing brain, I knew the purpose of hospice and came to understand how it works, but I had trouble translating that knowledge to my caregiving brain. Even though the switch to hospice was the right thing to do, the switch was emotionally difficult. Somehow using hospice was an acknowledgement that the end was at hand. I didn't want to give up, and it felt like contracting with hospice was giving up. I didn't want people to know that we were using it because I did not want it being said, as I have heard it said in hushed tones about other people, "They have called in hospice." Death for Kay was not imminent. It was just inevitable.

If Kay felt like we were giving up, she never expressed it. After I convinced her to try it, she never recoiled. She had to have known what it meant, but she once again demonstrated her emotional toughness and resilience.

Once we accepted our dependence on the hospice team and the absence of our previous team of physicians, we started to see advantages of the hospice program. First, we were no longer making trips to and from doctors' offices. We no longer had to see doctors, therapists, boxing instructors, or nurse practitioners. There was no point in seeing these people anymore. We could stay at home, and the medical attention would come to us.

A further benefit that we discovered very soon was that Medicare not only pays for the attention of the medical professionals on the care team, but also for the cost of all the medications related to the disease, all the medical equipment necessary to keep Kay comfortable, and all the incidentals, like adult diapers and bedsheets. There were no co-pays and no deductibles. Of course, Kay was not taking any medication for PSP, but she was taking a variety of RLS medications. All those medications, except the rotigotine patch, happened to be covered by the hospice formulary and wcrc made available to us without cost. Further, the medications, as well as adult diapers, bedsheets and other items that we needed to care for Kay, were delivered to our front door. We no longer needed to go to the drugstore. The medications she was taking for RLS, other than the patch, were not expensive, so we didn't realize a great financial advantage from the pharmaceutical part of the plan, but for someone in pain or otherwise in need of expensive medications, the benefit could be huge.

We did not take great advantage of the medical equipment that was available to us either. We were well fixed with wheelchairs. At one point, hospice brought a Hoyer Lift that the nurse thought might be useful in getting Kay in and out of bed. We found that it didn't work for us because of the configuration of our bed. A conventional hospital bed would have allowed us to use it properly, but neither Kay nor I wanted that. As previously mentioned, hospice did bring a hospital bed in the final days of her life. Alive, and all hospice providers, also have home health aides who would have come to our house to do basic care, but because we had Val and the other caregivers, I saw no need for the home health aides. We didn't take full advantage of all the hospice services, but for a terminally ill patient with limited resources and a limited support network, hospice would be a godsend. For us, hospice just made everything easier and less inconvenient.

All the nurses were excellent, very professional. It is a nursecentric operation. We never used the chaplain. In fact, Kay ran him off the only time he came. I was mortified. The social worker was quite helpful and was the one constant throughout hospice care. I met with her individually several times. She was even available for grief counseling after Kay died. She was the only one in the whole process who was willing to give me sad news when there was sad news to be given. By early spring, she was warning me in the most nurturing way that I should be prepared to lose Kay soon, even before Lauren and her family could return to Nashville from Australia in July. When Kay beat those odds, she told me to expect a fall-off after the emotion of Lauren's return and the celebration of our fiftieth anniversary. Kay fooled her both times, but at least she was willing to talk about it, which is what I needed.

When Kay died that fall afternoon, we immediately called the hospice nurse. The nurse and social worker arrived within minutes, and the nurse pronounced her dead. We had no EMTs trying to resuscitate her, no ambulance and fire trucks in the driveway, and no complications. It was a quiet, peaceful, dignified passing among family and friends. As horrible as her disease was, the passing was beautiful, facilitated in no small degree by hospice.

I had made arrangements with a funeral home in advance of the day of Kay's death. When the nurse came to our home and pronounced Kay dead, she called the funeral home herself and arranged for attendants to get Kay's body. The attendants arrived a couple of hours later, giving us time to be with Kay a little longer, and then took her away. The nurse and the social worker stayed with us through to the end until Kay left us. She died in her home, surrounded by the people who loved her the most, held in my arms, with all the medical attention that was needed close at hand. It was a very good way to die.

15

Lovegivers

*If I needed you, would you come to me? Would you come to
me and ease my pain*

"If I Needed You"—Townes Van Zandt

Kay and I were different in many ways. She was the extrovert who reveled in relationships. She loved people and could see straight through to their hearts. She was accepting of everyone, but she especially loved people with kind and true hearts, regardless of their economic, social, ethnic, educational, or other status in life. I am more introverted. I like people, too, and have a lot of friends, but I do not have her magnetism. Just as Kay absorbed energy by being with people, a cocktail party for me takes some effort. She was the social one. I like my space. You would always find her in a real or virtual clump of people. You might find me standing in a corner. Solitude gives me energy. Solitude made her restless. Seldom did a Friday or Saturday night pass when she did not have us engaged in some social endeavor. For her, it was always a delight. For me, not always. It was our disparate personalities that probably made us a good team. We each brought something different to the marriage.

We were also alike in many ways—driven, motivated, community-minded, and transparent in the way we lived our lives. This last one became especially important as Kay's illness progressed. We were open about everything. Our home was open to everyone, regardless who was there. Transparency also applied to the disease. I have already noted the emails that went out immediately upon our receiving the diagnosis. She said from the very beginning that she wanted everyone to know. Putting the story out there made a huge difference in how her friends could interact with her, how I could go about my life, and how she was able to relate to people. I think she was able to process the progression of the disease and the inevitability of it much better by processing it in the company of her caring coterie of friends rather than alone with her own thoughts. Kay was going to see her friends. That was a given. They were going to see her. By knowing the nature of the disease and how it would end, they became even more intentional about being with her, enjoying some good times and sharing their love.

There were very few days during her illness when we didn't have someone come and visit with Kay. I truly believe the social interaction she experienced throughout her illness extended her life. It made the life that she had left so much richer. For that, I will always be grateful and forever indebted to those people who came to see her day after day.

Pat and Bobby were the best of the love-giving best. As soon as Kay was diagnosed, Pat said, "I'm on this." And she was. She had recently wound down her marketing consulting practice, and she directed all that energy our way. Pat began mobilizing and organizing Kay's friends. At first, it was "Tuesdays with Kay" for as many of Kay's friends as could come visit with her at an appointed time on Tuesday afternoons. It became a community event with spirited conversation all around the room. Kay enjoyed it at first. It was convenient for her friends. They could come and go as their schedules allowed and still spend time with Kay. It also served as a big "Kay's world" convocation. People enjoyed seeing other people in Kay's orbit. Of course, Kay had been connecting people her whole life, so she was delighted.

As time wore on, "Tuesdays with Kay" became harder. Her speech difficulties prevented her from participating in the conversations. In that sort of gathering, there is a lot of overlapping, simultaneous, and impulsive conversation. Kay couldn't form her thoughts fast enough to participate, so she spent a lot of time listening, sitting on the periphery of her own party, like the girl at the dance with no date and no friends. Still, even when she could not participate, she enjoyed it for a time. Seeing people come together in her living room gave her satisfaction and joy. "Tuesdays with Kay" went on for a few months in the summer and fall of 2018. Finally, she told me that she wasn't enjoying it anymore, and we stopped doing it.

When "Tuesdays with Kay" became too much, Pat organized smaller group activities whereby two or three people would come at an appointed time and play Scrabble with Kay. She had always enjoyed board games, and Scrabble was a hit for a while. But soon, she was unable to do that anymore. Next, came Rummikub, the game previously mentioned played with tiles. Rummikub became her new obsession. But, eventually, she couldn't play Rummikub anymore. Pat then turned to organizing two-on-one visits and then one-on-one visits. To help us keep up with Kay's schedule, Pat and I shared a Google calendar. Her support went well beyond what sisters do for sisters. It was extraordinary.

Of all the extraordinary acts of kindness that Pat bestowed on us during Kay's illness, perhaps the most important, at least from my perspective, was Bobby's and her commitment to come, prepare and have dinner with us most nights, particularly once we found ourselves in the isolation of the COVID-19 quarantine. I have detailed how the afternoons and evenings could drag on interminably as the disease worsened, how I struggled to find things to occupy our time after PSP worsened when it was just the two of us, how hard it would sometimes be to combat restless legs in the afternoons, and how I would long for the presence of other people to make things a little easier. I came to anticipate Bobby and Pat's white Audi streaking past the dining room windows to their accustomed parking spot at six thirty each afternoon. I think Kay came to anticipate it as well. Interaction with other human beings was the solace we both needed. Yes, even I needed people.

For most of 2019, until the quarantine started in 2020, Kay would have a visitor in the morning and another visitor in the afternoon. Sometimes, it would be two to Kay's one and sometimes just one person with her. As she declined, she would get really tired by afternoon. Fatigue would bring on restless legs. So we began to restrict visits to mornings, although we weren't totally successful because so many of her friends wanted to see her. In a testimony to the circle of people who loved and cared for Kay throughout the ordeal and testimony to Kay's glorious spirit, they all said, without exception, that they looked forward to the visits. They didn't see the visits as a burden or a chore, nor did they see them as uncomfortable or awkward. They didn't see our house as a nursing home. They saw the visits as a privilege and joyful moment in their day.

When the pandemic quarantine set in for real in the spring of 2020, we had a few weeks of relative solitude. Val was still with us, and we were still seeing Jennifer and her family occasionally. Soon, Bobby and Pat started bringing dinner each night. But Lauren and her family were in Australia, and Barton and his family, pregnant with child, went into seclusion at our place in Rosemary Beach. It didn't take long before friends, who were willing to come to see Kay and wear a mask, started to re-emerge. People were thinking of us and instinctively knew that we couldn't survive with these twin diseases in total isolation. Continuing from mid-2020 and almost until her death, a different person or persons would come to read to her each day, seven days a week. By then, she had almost totally lost her ability to talk, so she would sit and listen. As 2021 unfolded and a reader would come, Kay might hang her head, and sometimes fall asleep. Our intrepid readers never wavered. They knew she might not be listening or comprehending, yet they kept coming, week after week. It was the presence of another loving human being that was important, not necessarily the book.

There were other friends who had their own niche. Elizabeth liked to get Kay out of the house. Kay needed that. Sometimes they would go shopping. Sometimes they would go somewhere for a walk. Sometimes they would just ride around. Val always went with them. I have described how Kay always came home with some discovered treasure from a shopping trip and the joy it gave her. Anne came for lunch every Friday even though neither Kay nor Anne ate lunch many of those days.

In the fall of 2020, I read Ann Patchett's article in *The New Yorker* about her three fathers and discovered that her father died of PSP. Ann is a friend of long-standing, but she wasn't a close enough friend to have known of Kay's struggle with PSP, and we certainly knew nothing of her father's diagnosis. I immediately sent Ann an email telling her I had read her essay and that Kay had PSP. From that point on, Ann was a constant. She would come and read to Kay also, but her readings might be a chapter from her forthcoming book, *These Precious Days*, or some other essay that was soon to be published. Ann knew what we were going through because she had been there with her father. She knew how bad it was and how bad it was going to be. She became a very good friend to both of us.

On most Saturdays we would have lunch with our friends Wally and LeeLee, and on Sundays with Gordon and Yvonne. There were other regulars at other times. There were many dinners. Kay's friend Linda, the mayoral candidate previously mentioned, came. Her mother died from PSP. She tried to help with advice born of experience. There were more, many more. I never really knew whether they were there to show their love for Kay or to take care of me. I had the support of my own friends as well. I have related how Joe and Don helped me through some the darkest days. I saw them over breakfast or lunch or on a walk once a week. Doug, our previously mentioned travel companion with his wife Sondra, was another guy friend in whom I could confide. All these people loved and sustained us. They brightened each day. I weep when I think of each one. We were blessed beyond our imagination.

Then there were our three children, their supportive spouses, and our nine healthy, happy grandchildren. From January 2018 until July 2021, Lauren and her family were in Australia. Kay's illness was probably harder on Lauren than anyone. She was so far away and could do so little to help. Her whole family came home for Christmas 2019. That was a wonderful treat. Kay was still healthy enough to enjoy that visit and be with her grandchildren. Lauren had planned to come home at three-month intervals to see and take care of Kay. Then COVID -19 came and Australia shut down. Even Australian citizens couldn't get in or out, and we didn't see her or her family for eighteen months. We would talk via FaceTime. Lauren sent us tons of pictures of the grandchildren. We used the internet app Marco Polo to pass videos and communicate across multiple time zones, but it was not the same as being together with them. Lauren must have felt so powerless. We were all powerless, but those of us who were with Kay had the power of the hug.

Barton's family was not thousands of miles away from us, but he and his family were limited because Hayley was pregnant with Tru. So little was known about the virus in the early days, Barton and Hayley took their family to Rosemary Beach and stayed in seclusion for several weeks in the early days of the pandemic. As previously mentioned, when Tru was born, her pediatrician cautioned against any contact outside the immediate family. That was hard for Kay. She wanted desperately to get her hands on her last grandchild to be born, her namesake, the baby she would never see grow up. Barton and Hayley did the best they could to let Kay see the baby while protecting her from who knows what peril in the days in which we knew so little about the disease.

Jennifer's family came every Sunday night for dinner. I think Sunday night dinners were her happiest times because she could see grand-children. Eventually, when Lauren's family came home and it was safer for Barton's family to see us, she was able to see all the grandchildren. Even in the last six months of her life, when she was really in decline, a grandchild walking in the door brought a glow to her face. She particu-larly yearned to see the little girls. She would grab a little hand and hold on for all she was worth. Even in her dying days, Kay had a firm grip. Sometimes we would have to pry her hand loose from a grandchild so he or she could go home. And the grandchildren were wonderful. They always had a hug for MomMom. I know Kay had to be a little bit scary in her diminished state, but they loved her. Jennifer's boys, who are older than the other grandchildren, probably now miss her the most because they had so much more time with her. She was blessed by the love of those kids. I think she knew she was blessed.

Jennifer, Lauren, and Barton were a support network for me. They all have their strengths, and I leaned on those strengths. Jennifer is the organizer and the planner. I needed her to help me navigate Kay's and my life, keep the household afloat, know where to go for resources and what to do in each unique circumstance of our life as it came up. She helped me find caregiving help. She connected me to hospice.

Lauren is a caregiver by nature. I could talk to her about how I felt, and she could help me with it. She is the one who sent me to the therapist. Even though she was miles and miles away, she worked hard at being a constant presence.

Barton seemed to have the most difficulty with his emotions. We all had our breakdowns, but as Kay grew worse, he was more fragile and had more overt breakdowns than Jennifer and Lauren. Even during the scariest COVID days when he and Hayley had to be especially careful, he would try to come by himself to see his mom. I needed all of them in their own special ways, and so did Kay.

We were also fortunate to have Kay's siblings. I have already praised Pat, but probably not as much as she deserves. Kay's older sister Susan lives in Louisville and owns an art gallery. She would come down when she could and spend several days at a time. She would pull me aside and bore in on my well-being. "How are you doing?" "You need rest." "You need to get away." For some reason, I found myself talking in a more personal way with her than with others in the family. When I went to Rosemary in September of 2020, Susan seemed to be the most persuasive in getting Kay to acquiesce to my going, although Kay was never thrilled about it. Susan and Pat organized a three-day party for Kay while I was away, including a music night with the singer/song-writer, Marshall Chapman, and a pool party at Gordon and Yvonne's where the virtually voiceless Kay was captured on video belting out the national anthem. Toward the end, Kay's sister-in-law Cathy came many days in the afternoon in that dreaded three to six thirty slot to give me some company. In the end, Kay's brothers, Don and Tom, were there to mourn and share the pain.

Finally, she had me. I tried my best. I was not always present the way she wanted, and I could have done more. But I loved her and I do love her, and she intensely loved me. I felt so sorry for her. I wanted to do anything I could to make her life better. We had the special closeness of fifty years of commitment to each other, and that commitment and closeness sustained us. But our married life was not perfect. Things didn't always go well. We disagreed and came in conflict with each other. I am not by nature an emotive person, and in our everyday life, she didn't always get the demonstrable expressions of love from me that she wanted. Not that she was clingy. To the contrary, she was independent, but she saw marriage as a sharing of every aspect of our lives. For me, I sometimes wanted my own space. We would clash and disagree, but love, commitment, trust, attachment, and intimacy would always win out. The intimacy of marriage bonded us and connected us emotionally. It reassured both of us of our mutual love and commitment. Those moments said to me that she loved me deeply and passionately, and I think it said the same to her. I am so thankful for that foundation we built over all our years together.

I think often about people who contract PSP or any terminal, chronic, torturous disease, who are not surrounded by lovegivers like we were. We had a few periods of isolation—the COVID quarantine, Val's absence nursing her own bout with COVID, and the exile imposed by a snow and ice storm. The days crept by during those times, but we had each other, and there was a precious quality to that. We had always taken care of each other and we still were. And then, when we needed the presence of others, they were there. They were there in extraordinary abundance and quality of service to our needs. What we had in those three and half years was extraordinary in every way.

16

Grief

I'd walk all the way from Boulder to Birmingham if I thought I could
see your face

"Boulder to Birmingham"—Emmylou Harris

What is grief? Is it missing someone that you know will never be with you again, at least not in a way we understand? Is it pity and sorrow for that one who can no longer experience this world? Is it somehow narcissistic, reminding us that we too are mortal, that life is finite and it is fragile? Is it loneliness? Is it not having that person to talk to? Is it not having that person to share your thoughts and emotions with? Is it regret for not having been a more loving loved one, wanting a "do over"? Is it wanting to undo what death has wrought? Grief is a trip to your innermost feelings and emotions. Grief is crying. Grief is painful, deeply painful.

Before Kay died, I had moments when I wished for her death. She was in such a miserable place. She couldn't do anything, say anything, or enjoy anything. I thought I would be relieved when the end came. I thought watching this beautiful person waste away would be much worse than dealing with her loss. In those final days, I wrote the following, trying to unload and unpack what I was feeling:

> *I know that this cannot go on much longer. She is so frail. She is not eating. She barely expels anything from her body. Yet, she holds on. Out of determination, physical core strength? I don't know. She is asleep now after a hard day of battling her legs and PSP fatigue, yet it is only 5:00 p.m. How much longer can this go on? I look at her wheelchair, the one she has lived in almost constantly for well over a year, and I want it to go away. I want this to be over. She is suffering, her friends are suffering, her family is suffering. Yet, she will not give up. It is as if the disease is telling her, "I am not through with you yet. You are mine and I will make your life miserable." Then, I feel guilty, thinking that I want it to be over. It is easier to say "I want it to be over" than to say "I want her to die." She is a living, breathing human being whom I love. She knows her surroundings. She knows what is going on around her. I don't want that to stop, for her sake. The line between life and death is not a narrow line—it is a chasm. Living is living, no matter the difficulties. Dying is forever. Living is what we do. It is what we know. Dying is a mystery, and it is so final. So I don't want her to die and I don't want her to live if living is what it is now. It is the emotional miasma of the moment.*

The hospice people said she could still hear and comprehend until the very end. I could talk to her, as could others, and presumably she would understand, still be a part of this world. She could watch, or hear, *Breakfast at Tiffany's* that last night. But then death came, and she was no longer with us. Her physical presence, as heartbreaking as it was, was no longer with us. Could I still talk to her and her soul be present to hear it? I don't know. No one knows.

Joan Didion in *The Year of Magical Thinking*—her book about the loss of her husband, John Dunne— recounts the time immediately after his death when she could not accept it, thought she could change it, kept thinking she could somehow magically bring him back, would not publish an obituary because then the world would know and it would be final. Death is final. It is irreversible. I think that is why it is so hard. Joan Didion couldn't bring her husband back. We think we can fix everything if we try hard enough, but we can't fix death.

Alan Lightman in his book, *Searching for Stars on an Island in Maine,* postulates that upon death, the atoms that compose the matter we call a human body simply disperse into the universe and perhaps hover over those places of love and belonging. According to Lightman, matter does not disappear. It transforms. I don't know whether I believe Lightman's construct or not, but I choose to think about Kay's death in that way. I want to believe that her atoms and her being are still around and inhabit those special places. Maybe those atoms take the form of fairies or angels or some other magical being. I choose to think about death that way. I need to think about it that way. Otherwise, what do I have to hold onto? If we apply Lightman's theory, maybe the difference between life and death is not a chasm, but a very thin line. Maybe she is still with us in her own new transcendent presence.

The corollary to death and grieving is loneliness. Under normal circumstances, I don't mind being alone. There are many times when I rather like it. One night soon after she died, I watched an episode of *This Is Us* in which Jack's mother dies. Jack is one of the main characters. He had had a tough childhood and a difficult relationship with his father. His mother had been abused by his father. He loved his mother, but he had shut her out of his life along with all the memories of his youth. He had not seen her in thirteen years. He said he had been too busy. At the episode ended, I wanted to talk to Kay about it. But she was not present. She was not there. I had no one to talk to. I have friends and family and even a therapist, if I choose to use her, but I can't talk to anyone in the same way Kay and I talked.

At times, I want to scream, "Come back. I need you!" I do need her. We were both independent personalities, but we needed each other. We both knew that. I needed her because I could talk to her, confide in her like no one else. I need her now. I have no one I can talk to in the ways I could talk to her. "Come back. I need you!"

I have thought a lot about whether I was a good husband. Had I been neglectful? Yes, sometimes. Whether from laziness or distraction or ego-absorption or emotions withheld, I could have been better. She deserved better. She loved me. I hope she felt loved. Did she know how much I loved her? Of all the subsets of grief, the one that haunts me the most is whether I was good enough as a husband, not just as a caregiver at the end, but as a husband and a friend for over fifty years. I could have done more. I could have been more present. I could have expressed my love more tenderly and more often. I think about it all the time.

She couldn't say in those last hours how she felt. She was deprived of last words. She would have said she loved me. She would have said she loved her family and her friends, each in a special way. I know that. What I don't know is whether she would have said, "I am loved. I am at peace." We will never know whether she was content when she died, whether she was at peace, and, most importantly, whether she felt loved. Not knowing is hard.

For the first two weeks after Kay's death, I engaged in a lot of activity and social interaction. The activities distracted me from thinking about her constantly. It was almost as though she was away for a few days and would soon return. When I arose on Thanksgiving morning, just two weeks following her death, I vowed to give thanks all day for Kay. I talked to Karen and Rob. I talked to Val. I texted with some friends. I said the same thing to everyone. Let's give thanks for Kay, for her long and productive life, and the time we had with her. Then I started missing her and needing her and knowing that I could never have her with me again. I don't see that life is going to be anything of joy, just doing it by myself. It is so hard to accept that she is gone, and will never come back.

On December 29, 2021, slightly more than a month after she died, I had a dream. I dreamed that Kay and Brant, a former law partner before I retired, got into an argument. Brant is a generation younger than me and someone for whom I have great respect and admiration, but I have no explanation as to his presence in my dream. Both Kay and Brant had guns, and as they argued, they shot each other. I saw it happen and could do nothing to stop it. I seemed frozen in place watching the scene play out. No one else seemed to see it or know anything about it. I told everyone I could tell, but no one seemed to care. Kay was dead. I don't remember about Brant, but I don't think he fared well either. Then, in my dream, I went to bed. When I awoke the next morning, still in my dream, Pat and Cathy were with me, and I said, "Did you hear about Kay?" They said no. I told them what had happened. They said, "What are you talking about? She is right here." I turned and looked, and there she was. I grabbed her and held her tight for the longest time. I noticed, however, that she was wearing a blue patterned top and a red patterned skirt that didn't match. She would never have dressed like that. Then I woke up. That is the last time I have seen her.

Soon after the first of the year, I went to our house in Rosemary Beach for solitude and reflection. I was in Rosemary when I wrote most of this. Kay was all around me there. She'd designed everything when we built the house. She had kept it current through the years with wall hangings, art, landscaping, floor coverings, kitchen appliances and utensils, and anything else that makes a house a home. She was talented in so many ways. She noticed things I didn't notice, can't notice, and then she would say, "We have to fix this or that or replace this or that or add to this or that," and I would say, "Don't you think it is just fine the way it is?" I would always lose that argument. She was always right.

I rode her bike one day while in Rosemary, the same one from which she fell, starting us on this journey now concluded. The bike is a really nice multispeed that she hoped to ride for a long time. The pump sitting beside it was built to last a lifetime. The couches in the house were purchased and placed according to her specifications. The storage room is stocked with bicycles, skateboards, tools for building sandcastles at the beach, baby beds, and a video game console. Everything there is there in anticipation of a long life enjoying grandchildren, friends, the beach, the sun, and the ocean. It is all there the way she wanted it, and the way she was going to enjoy it for many years to come. But she didn't get those years. She got, instead, a death much too early. She got a death that didn't even give her the privilege of last words.

Missing her was worse at Rosemary than at our home in Nashville. I don't know why. Maybe it is because her illness had been so prolonged and the consequences so profound that, in many ways, I started thinking of the house in which she died as a house without her. In Rosemary, my memories were of her the way she was. Rosemary was our sanctuary, the place that our family—the children, their spouses, and their children—could all go and be under one roof. The grandchildren bonded and loved being with each other when they were there. Kay was in the middle of all of that and loved it there. Being there alone all winter made me miss her in a more profound and intense way. It seemed understandable that she wasn't at our home in Nashville. She departed the world there. It was her launching pad into the next world. But, at Rosemary, she was still alive, but missing.

One night at Rosemary, I sat alone on the balcony of our house looking at the sunset wishing she was there, crying my eyes out. Joan Didion said in *The Year of Magical Thinking* that grief is different from mourning. I think her characterization is that grief is received, it is passive, whereas mourning is active. Mourning is the act of dealing with grief. Mourning is the act of moving forward, getting over grief. I am not saying it as well as she said it, but I know that I was sitting there on the balcony in the dark, thinking all these thoughts, writing them down, and weeping, crying, bawling, not able to stop. I have received grief and found mourning. I think I would rather find Kay and be together again so we could talk like we did fifty-plus years ago at the University of Kentucky's campus and like we did not so long ago.

17

In Memoriam

She's gone away in yesterday
Now I find myself on the mountainside
Where the rivers change direction
Across the great divide

"Across the Great Divide"—Kate Wolf

What does it feel like when you know you are going to die? On June 7, 2018, Kay knew she was going to die. She didn't know when, but she knew it was coming as sure as dark follows light. She knew she wasn't going to see her grandchildren grow into adulthood. She knew she might never even meet all her grandchildren. What was on her mind? We cried that day. But then she pulled it together and continued to do so every single day for the next three and a half years.

In *For Whom the Bell Tolls*, Ernest Hemingway's character Sordo is a guerrilla fighter against the nationalist forces of Francisco Franco in the Spanish Civil War. When Sordo finds himself and his band of fighters surrounded by the nationalist army, he knows death is imminent. As he lies on a mountain hillside surrounded by the enemy, Hemingway reflects on death through Sordo:

Dying was nothing and he had no picture of it nor fear
of it in his mind. But living was a field of grain blowing

in the wind on the side of a hill. Living was a hawk in the
sky. Living was an earthen jar of water in the dust of the
threshing with the grain flailed out and the chaff blowing.
Living was a horse between your legs and a carbine under
one leg and a hill and a valley and a stream with trees along
it and the far side of the valley and the hills beyond.

Sordo did not fear death, but he loved life. I don't think Kay
feared death, but she loved life.

Kay was a woman of purpose. She lived life to the fullest, and as
she declined in health, she had no intentions of letting the disease rob
her of a life of purpose. She deserved to live. When friends would come
to see her and walk in the front door and ask her how she was doing,
she would always say, or try to say, "Great." She had to be really sad
on the inside, but she didn't want to make any of her guests sad. Even
in her dying days, she was visiting and corresponding with Andrew, the
death row inmate she had befriended. She was still trying to take care
of others, knowing full well that she was dying, knowing full well she
couldn't take care of any of us much longer, but still trying. It was in
her soul—helping others and welcoming her guests into her home.

I wanted to help her, but I didn't know what to do. We tried to be
normal, but I don't know whether that was good enough. We weren't
normal. She was dying, and we were dying, just one small drip at a time
from the faucet until the kettle was full and could hold no more–at
which point she could only lie in the arms of the people who loved her
the most and go away.

As I write, I know that she still lives. She lives in my heart and in the
hearts of so many others. The disease took her life. In a sense, it won.
But in a sense it didn't. She got her licks in. She never lost her smile or
the light in her eyes. She never ceased to brighten up when her grandchildren came around. Even on her last night, mute, emaciated, staring
into the unknown, she watched, or maybe just listened to, *Breakfast
at Tiffany's*. She died as she lived, with class and joy in the life she
had lived.

She kept her apprehension of death bottled up. In her mind, she didn't need, nor want, the hospice chaplain nor the therapist nor the priest for pastoral care. She didn't want to unpack emotions. She had it under control. She wanted everything in her life to be under control, including the way she would deal with the disease. She had her tears, but considering what a prolonged and brutal illness she had, her tears were few indeed. She had an incredible unwavering ability throughout her life to transcend obstacles and live her life to the fullest. She continued to do so even in the face of death.

In those three and a half years of knowing her fate, Kay was obsessed about not being forgotten. It was as if she latched onto that emotion and used it as a proxy for living. It seemed that she could accept death as long as she was not going to be forgotten. After Kay died, someone said to me Kay was the most complex personality that person had ever known. I never thought of her as complex. She was certainly a handful. She was unique and extraordinary, but was she complex? I have to think about that. But, she will never be forgotten.

I have spent countless hours since Kay died working on this narrative. I have never done anything like this. At times, I asked myself why this manuscript was so important to me that I would devote so many hours to it. The answer is, I just felt compelled to do it. I had no choice. Something was in me that had to come out. I didn't want what Kay went through, what all of us who cared for her and loved her went through, to be forgotten. It had to be preserved. I didn't want to bury the experience. I don't want it to be forgotten, just like I don't want her to be forgotten.

I started writing even before Kay died, hoping it would be cathartic for me. I was looking for a positive way to deal with the exhaustion of caregiving and the grief of loss. I also hoped the many people who loved Kay would read this and would find it cathartic for them as well. Since Kay's death, her friends have said things to me like "I think of her every day" or "I cannot walk through your front door without feeling sad" or

"I miss her so." I hope what I have done here will help bring peace and closure for all of us who loved her and still love her.

My writing of this, the reflection, and the rewriting has taken me to the month of April, almost five months since losing her. Spring is mounting a frontal assault and losing. Winter is a formidable foe. But I know that spring will prevail. It is unrelenting, and in another two weeks, we will be enveloped by blooms and baby leaves. As the months have gone by, I have healed some. I still miss her a lot and probably always will, but spring will come.

What I have written and my experience in writing it is perhaps a start on a new life for me and maybe for our whole family and her many friends. As we all start that new life without her, it must be a life that we live in her honor, filled with her love, her caring regard for all people, and her love of life. For me, I have vowed to try to live the rest of my days as a more empathetic, more caring, more loving, less judgmental person, asking always in all things, "What would Kay do?"

My sincerest thanks go to three of my good friends who graciously served as readers of the first draft of Losing Kay. Don Welch is mentioned with affection in the book as one of my spiritual guides in the darkest days. He and Kay were professional colleagues at Vanderbilt Law School in Nashville for many years. Don knew Kay as well as anyone, bringing a unique perspective to his reading.

Paul Wagner has known Kay and me for over 50 years. He was one of my closest friends in college and the best man in our wedding. Paul is a documentary filmmaker living in Charlottesville, Virginia, with his wife, Ellen. He added the perspective of someone who knew both Kay and me but also is a professional storyteller.

Susan Lanigan is a lawyer. She and I met when we served on a board together. She was a steadfast luncheon companion through the tough days of my worry about Kay and stress over her illness. She brought the perspective of someone who never knew Kay and could read unencumbered by past experience with our family. She was a very meticulous reader.

The final edit was done by Pat Peters. I was a law school classmate of her husband Steve at Vanderbilt Law School. Pat and Kay became good friends during our law school days and remained so over the ensuing years. Pat went on to have a successful career as a book editor. Her professional expertise was invaluable in turning my manuscript into a publishable piece.

I am deeply grateful to all four of these good friends.

Keith Simmons is retired from the practice of law. He and Kay met in college, were married soon after her graduation and remained married for over fifty years. They have three children and nine grandchildren, all of whom live in Nashville ten minutes from Kay and Keith's home. Keith is a graduate of the University of Kentucky and Vanderbilt Law School.